Contributions to Management Science

AF828830

The series *Contributions to Management Science* contains research publications in all fields of business and management science. These publications are primarily monographs and multiple author works containing new research results, and also feature selected conference-based publications are also considered. The focus of the series lies in presenting the development of latest theoretical and empirical research across different viewpoints.

This book series is indexed in Scopus.

More information about this series at http://www.springer.com/series/1505

Wolfgang Stoelzle • Julia Burkhardt
Editors

# Sub-Supplier Management

## A Buyer-Centric, Low-Tier Supply Chain Perspective

Springer

*Editors*
Wolfgang Stoelzle
ISCM-HSG
University of St. Gallen
St. Gallen, Switzerland

Julia Burkhardt
ISCM-HSG
University of St. Gallen
St. Gallen, Switzerland

ISSN 1431-1941 ISSN 2197-716X (electronic)
Contributions to Management Science
ISBN 978-3-030-75577-5 ISBN 978-3-030-75575-1 (eBook)
https://doi.org/10.1007/978-3-030-75575-1

© The Editor(s) (if applicable) and The Author(s), under exclusive license to Springer Nature Switzerland AG 2021
This work is subject to copyright. All rights are solely and exclusively licensed by the Publisher, whether the whole or part of the material is concerned, specifically the rights of translation, reprinting, reuse of illustrations, recitation, broadcasting, reproduction on microfilms or in any other physical way, and transmission or information storage and retrieval, electronic adaptation, computer software, or by similar or dissimilar methodology now known or hereafter developed.
The use of general descriptive names, registered names, trademarks, service marks, etc. in this publication does not imply, even in the absence of a specific statement, that such names are exempt from the relevant protective laws and regulations and therefore free for general use.
The publisher, the authors, and the editors are safe to assume that the advice and information in this book are believed to be true and accurate at the date of publication. Neither the publisher nor the authors or the editors give a warranty, expressed or implied, with respect to the material contained herein or for any errors or omissions that may have been made. The publisher remains neutral with regard to jurisdictional claims in published maps and institutional affiliations.

This Springer imprint is published by the registered company Springer Nature Switzerland AG.
The registered company address is: Gewerbestrasse 11, 6330 Cham, Switzerland

# About the Book

This book is the outcome of an Innosuisse-based research project between 2015 and 2017 at the Institute of Supply Chain Management, University of St. Gallen (ISCM-HSG). We would like to deeply thank Innosuisse, as it was only due to their generous funding that we were able to execute a practical-oriented research project with four Swiss business partners. Furthermore, we would like to thank Coop, Rieter, SBB and Weleda for their time and dedication towards the topic of sub-supplier management. Through their insights and time, we were able to lay the foundation of the upcoming topic of sub-supplier management. Furthermore, we would like to thank Leon Klose who, with his eye for detail and continuous effort during the editing of the book, highly contributed to the finalization of the book project.

The book will give you an overview of the status quo in sub-supplier management. You will gain insights into relationship constellations between the buyer and the sub-supplier. If you are interested in implementing sub-supplier management at your company, it will give you hands-on advice on managing sub-suppliers in your supply chain and it will shed light on capabilities that are required at a buyer and sub-supplier level to make working together a success. Furthermore, you will learn how sub-supplier management can positively contribute to sustainability in your supply chain. Additionally, you will discover how digitalization can positively influence insights into your supply chain including sub-supplier management.

Enjoy our insights how to successfully manage sub-suppliers and start to make your supply chain more transparent, resilient and sustainable.

# About the Book

# Contents

# Contributors

**Elisabeth Altmayer** Institute of Supply Chain Management, University of St. Gallen, St. Gallen, Switzerland

**Julia Burkhardt** Institute of Supply Chain Management, University of St. Gallen, St. Gallen, Switzerland

**Hedwig Maria Scharlipp** ecos, Basel, Switzerland

**Ingo Schönwandt** University of St. Gallen, St. Gallen, Switzerland

**Alissa Schwarz** Weleda, Schwäbisch Gmünd, Germany

**Carsten Vollrath** SWISS IPG Partners Group AG, Zurich, Switzerland

# Status Quo in Sub-supplier Management

**Elisabeth Altmayer**

**Abstract** Today's supply chain managers are more and more confronted with challenges and risks arising from their indirect lower-tier suppliers. In this chapter, an overview over the status quo of sub-supplier management is given. A step-by-step analysis of current and future issues is introduced and used to evaluate the challenges and risks of a European airplane manufacturer's supply chains. Furthermore, a multistep analysis for the description of supply chain objectives impacted by sub-suppliers is explained and executed on the example of a sub-supplier project initiative of a Swiss-based watch manufacturer.

Today's supply chain managers are more and more confronted with challenges arising not from their direct suppliers but from their indirect lower-tier suppliers. When starting to engage in a comprehensive approach in sub-supplier management, the particular challenges a firm is facing due to its sub-suppliers should be evaluated. For the further practical approach of these challenges, they have to be compared and later aligned with supply chain management as well as the firm's general objectives.

## 1 Challenges and Risks Induced Through Sub-suppliers

When aiming at addressing specific sub-supplier-induced challenges within a company, a three-step analysis is appropriate, evaluating challenges caused by sub-suppliers and objectives impacted by sub-suppliers and linking those together for prioritization of sub-supplier-induced challenges based on costs and benefits of addressing each challenge (Fig. 1).

E. Altmayer (✉)
Institute of Supply Chain Management, University of St. Gallen, St. Gallen, Switzerland
e-mail: elisabeth.altmayer@unisg.ch

© The Author(s), under exclusive license to Springer Nature Switzerland AG 2021 
W. Stoelzle, J. Burkhardt (eds.), *Sub-Supplier Management*, Contributions to Management Science, https://doi.org/10.1007/978-3-030-75575-1_1

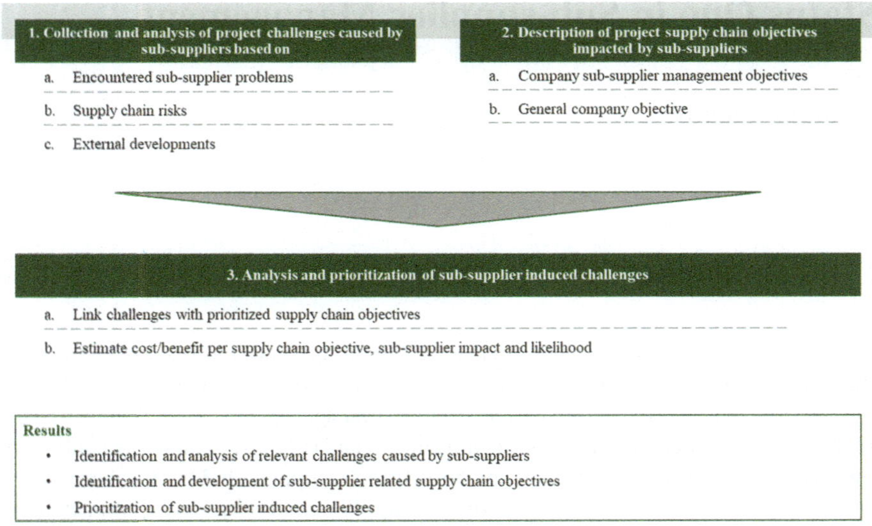


**Fig. 1** Analysis of challenges caused by sub-suppliers. Source: Authors' own illustration

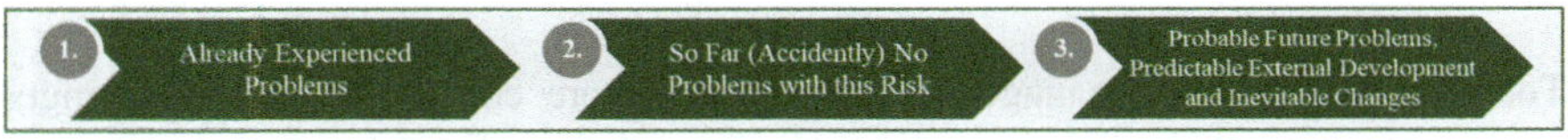


**Fig. 2** Steps in sub-supplier risk evaluation. Source: Authors' own illustration

## *1.1 A Step-by-Step Analysis of Current and Future Issues*

At the beginning of the investigation, challenges caused by sub-suppliers are evaluated. This evaluation contains three categories:

1. Encountered sub-supplier problems in the past
2. Supply chain risk
3. External developments with anticipated effect on own supply chain (Fig. 2)

## *1.2 A Broad Range of Typical Issues with Sub-suppliers*

Exemplary already encountered sub-supplier problems for many companies are topics like the lack of influence on sub-supplier level, the lack of supply chain transparency, the usage of material opposing to strategic goal of sustainability, the lack of standardization (of processes, process instructions, or IT infrastructure), the low supply reliability of (sub-)suppliers, problems caused by single sourcing, or the lack of communication (internal as well as external) (Yan et al. 2015) (Fig. 3).

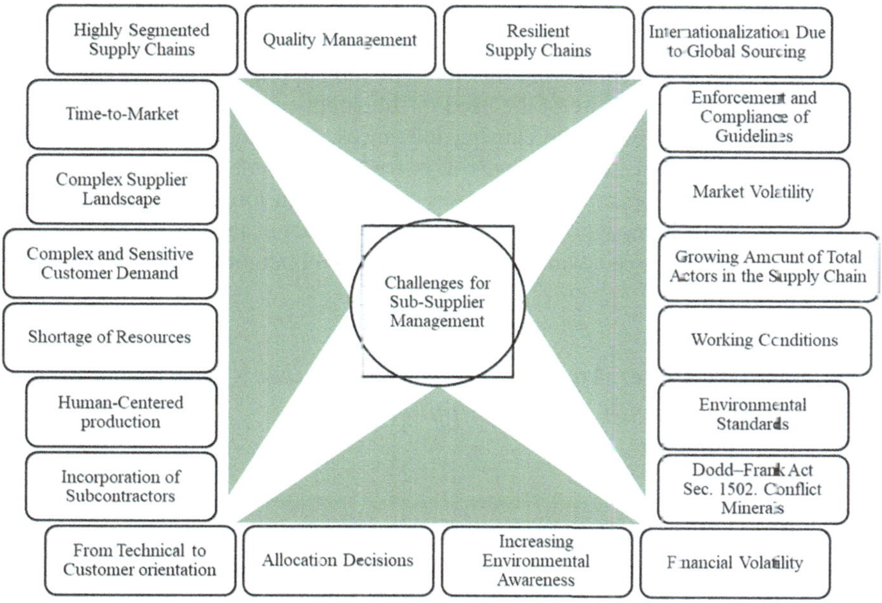


**Fig. 3** Selected challenges induced through sub-suppliers in practice. Source: Authors' own illustration

## *1.3 Supply Chain Risks: Extending the Scope of a Familiar Approach*

When evaluating current supply chain risks, companies are facing permanent threats due to single sourcing (caused by stringent specification), country-specific risks, lack of transparency and knowledge regarding sub-suppliers (e.g., unknown degree of compliance), lack of communication on sub-supplier level (tier 1 to tier-2), reluctance of suppliers to provide information (on sub-suppliers) poor control and monitoring systems, and that a (sub-)supplier is incapable of fulfilling performance requirements and standards (e.g., quality, quantity) and therefore threatens the supply chain performance and supply security.

## *1.4 Future External Developments and Their Effect on a Company's Supply Chain*

Consideration of future external events anticipated to have an impact of a firms supply chain often involves topics like volatile prices and costs in foreign countries, e.g., due to punitive tariffs, increasing requirements concerning transparency formulated by government, customer and media, an increasingly complex and unpredictable procurement market, unstable governmental regulations, and changing customer demands.

Immediately after encountering hits through sub-supplier-induced challenges, a firm's attention is most aware of the need of sub-supplier management and is eager to engage in elimination of the causing influences. Nevertheless, considering the three different categories of challenges, it is crucial to enable a firm to proactively avoid or reduce the impact of future crises originating in lower-tier supply chains. Furthermore, actively recognizing future problems affecting an entire industry might also lead to a competitive advantage towards main competitors.

## *1.5 Industry Case: An Airplane Manufacturer's Specific Challenges with Its Sub-suppliers*

### 1.5.1 Background

The main objective for the airplane manufacturer is ensuring quality and quantities throughout its supply chains. The company is European based and produces small airplanes (private and military jets). Supply chains run global, with a significant hub of sub-suppliers located in the USA. Due to its size, the company is in a weaker position in case of supply shortages, when suppliers instead guarantee quantities for the major airplane manufacturers. The exceptional security standards of the industry requirements are that every single part used in production needs to be regulated, tested, and officially approved—a process that can take up to 5 years for every innovation or change in specification.

### 1.5.2 Sub-supplier Challenges Encountered in the Past

The company experienced material shortages or quality concerns due to sub-suppliers (they account for 80 % of the cases). However, the exact sub-suppliers causing issues could not be identified, since the manufacturer has no transparency in regard to where the issues arise precisely beyond its direct suppliers. Another challenge is that any indirect approaches to managing sub-suppliers are blocked by direct suppliers, who do not pass on information.

### 1.5.3 General Risks in Supply Chains, not Encountered so Far

Certain sub-supplier parts are used in the majority of the manufacturer's airplane models. If their supply would run short, there is a high risk for the overall turnover of the company. Although the parts themselves are not the most valuable in purchasing volume, shortage or long-term quality issues within the respective supply chains could severely damage the manufacturer.

Another permanent risk within the industry is that a competitor acquires a relevant innovation through one of its (sub-)suppliers, to which the manufacturer, in this case, would not have any access. Due to the long accreditation processes for new parts, any competitor would have a long-term competitive advantage that could push out all other competitors within a segment for up to 5 years.

#### 1.5.4 External Developments with the Anticipated Effect on the Supply Chain

Since supply chains in the industry are globally scattered, any global risk originating in political, economic, or social crises can threaten availability of the supplied parts (e.g., Israel, Russia, Ukraine).

## 2 Towards a Project Initiative in Sub-supplier Management

### *2.1 Creating Momentum for Sub-supplier Management*

Addressing sub-supplier-induced challenges mostly happens through project-based initiatives. For internal approval and insurance of commitment, challenges should be linked with concrete supply chain management objectives further than just the objectives of reducing a specific sub-supplier issue (Fig. 4).

When describing supply chain objectives impacted by sub-suppliers, again a processual multistep analysis is recommended. Starting with a project-centric collection of objectives to be addressed with a sub-supplier management project, further additional potential general objectives for the firm are collected to ensure non-conflicts. These objectives are then specified and prioritized based on budget and time constraints, resulting in a (list of) focused objectives for a sub-supplier management project initiative.

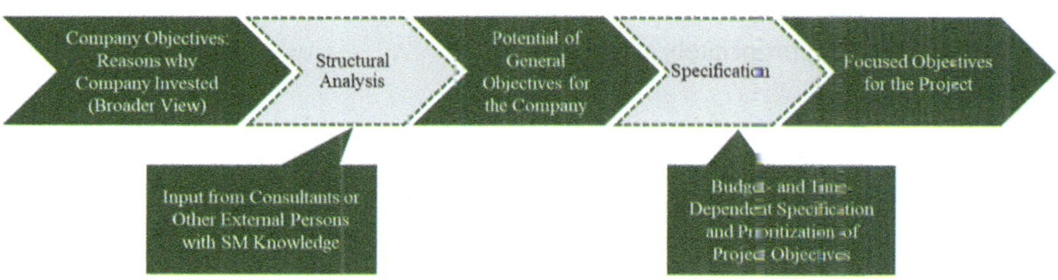


**Fig. 4** Creating momentum for sub-supplier management. Source: Authors' own illustration

## 2.2 *Objectives for Companies to Engage in a Sub-supplier Management Project Initiative*

Exemplary company objectives for participating in a sub-supplier management project-initiative are the need for identification of critical (sub-)suppliers and creation of supply chain transparency, increase productivity, efficiency, quality, safety, sustainability, and supply reliability of specific sub-suppliers. Furthermore, supply chain management usually desires the development of competencies and a management approach to deal with sub-suppliers, identify current relationship type, and, if necessary, adapt/shift to a more favorable relationship type and build a general understanding of sub-supplier management as a concept.

## 2.3 *Creating a Broader Picture: Adding a General Supply Chain or Company Objectives*

Afterwards, a structural analysis is conducted, where input from consultants and external persons with SM knowledge is collected, which results in general objectives for the project. The main topics help in identifying sub-suppliers beyond known system suppliers, generically applicable approaches for management of sub-suppliers, provision of case studies and standard operating procedures for sub-supplier management, integration of project results with risk analysis, identification of black boxes, and transparency of buyer requirements within supply chains.

## 2.4 *Consideration of Time and Budget Constraints*

Utilizing the general firm's objectives as an orientation, these topics are now prioritized, considering budget and time constraints. This results in specific sub-supplier management project objectives such as establishing supply chain transparency, shortening the time-to-market of new developments, proactively ensuring credibility, minimizing the risk of loss of company reputation, and ensuring suppliers and sub-suppliers comply with requirements, and cases of poor compliance will be processed appropriately.

## 2.5 Case: Specific Objectives for Sub-supplier Project Initiative from a Swiss-Based Watch Manufacturer

### 2.5.1 Background

The main performance objectives in the watch manufacturer's supply chains are quality and availability. By estimation, one-third to one-half of the problems related to quality and availability arise at the sub-supplier level. Due to lack of transparency, the exact number of cases in which problems are caused by sub-suppliers beyond the first-tier level is difficult to specify for the firm. While a formal procurement guideline exists, distinctive principles for achieving the objectives throughout the supply chain (i.e., at supplier and sub-supplier level) are neither integrated at the strategic nor at the operative level. The communication with sub-suppliers occurs occasionally and reactively on a case-by-case basis.

### 2.5.2 Objectives for Sub-supplier Management Projects

The manufacturer aims at extending the existing supplier management processes so that the main performance objectives can be ensured both at the supplier and sub-supplier level. This shall be done on a case-by-case basis, yet in future proactively (i.e., before undesired events occur). The primary responsibilities and structures for achieving the objectives throughout the supply chain are rooted in the procurement department, ensuring coordination between departments (e.g., design, procurement, construction, and quality) whenever necessary.

Measurable objectives are:

- Higher efficiency (i.e., additional benefits and fewer costs)
- More excellent safety concerning the availability of supplies (in general) and brand reputation (sustainability of sourced leather)
- Higher speed related to problem resolution/prevention (e.g., supply bottlenecks) and innovative capacity, especially in cases when new (and often small) product lines are launched

For all tasks going beyond the mandate of purchasing, the establishment of a specific cross-functional committee or council for integrated conflict resolution is advisable. This council should consist of purchasing, marketing, production, and quality executives. It should meet regularly, apply specified processes, and ensure follow-up.

### 2.5.3 Matching Challenges and Objectives and Building a Business Case

At first, each earlier defined challenge is linked with specific project objectives. Afterwards, the challenges are prioritized by their contribution to fulfilling the

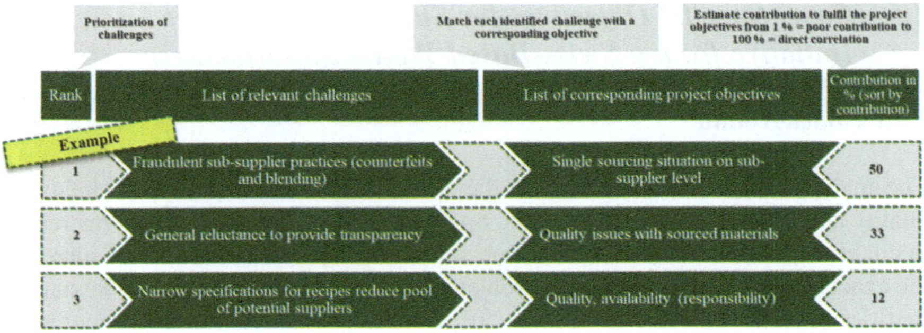


**Fig. 5** Linking challenges with prioritized supply chain objectives. Source: Authors' own illustration

project objectives (1% = weak contribution, 100% = direct correlation). This is applied to find the corresponding sub-supplier management processes to improve or implement. Figure 5 illustrates an exemplary match of challenges and objectives for a sub-supplier management project within the cosmetics industry:

Exemplary already encountered sub-supplier problems for many companies are topics like the lack of influence on sub-supplier level, the lack of supply chain transparency, the usage of material opposing to strategic goal of sustainability, the lack of standardization (of processes, process instructions, or IT infrastructure), the low supply reliability of (sub-)suppliers, problems caused by single sourcing, or the lack of communication (internal as well as external).

### 2.5.4 Building a Business Case for Sub-supplier Management to Ensure Project Funds and Commitment

In many cases, after the definition of the project scope and objectives, a project team might require for (additional) funding of a respective project initiative to be pursued. Conduction of a scenario-based business case is an appropriate method to demonstrate cost of non-action as well as potential benefits of actively engaging in sub-supplier management activities.

Within the business case calculation, the four dimensions are cost caused by sub-supplier incidents, cost reduction through effective sub-supplier management, decrease in turnover due to sub-supplier incidents, and increase in turnover due to effective sub-supplier management, calculated in two scenarios of an optimistic and a pessimistic outcome. The following illustration provides an exemplary processual approach (Fig. 6).

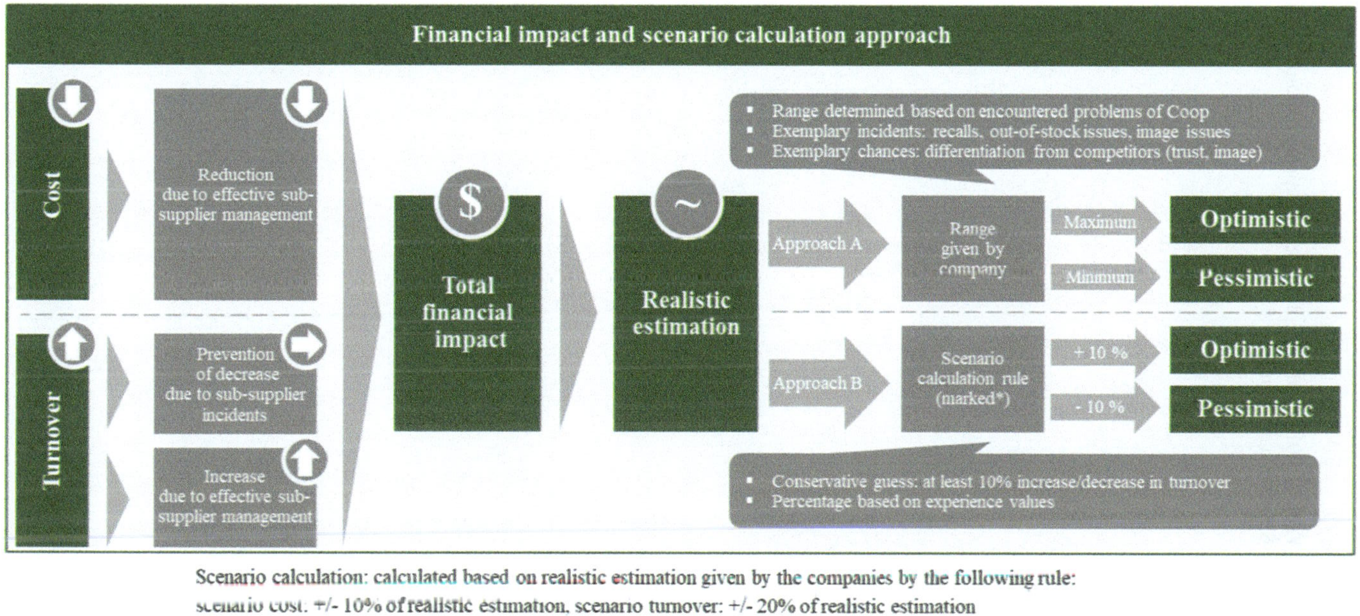


**Fig. 6** Estimating financial impact in scenarios. Source: Authors' own illustration

## Reference

Yan T, Choi TY, Kim Y, Yang Y (2015) A theory of the nexus supplier: a critical supplier from a network perspective. J Supply Chain Manag 51:52–66

# Buyer-Sub-supplier Relationships

**Elisabeth Altmayer and Ingo Schönwandt**

**Abstract** Engaging in sub-supplier management activities requires insights into characteristics and dynamics of a firm's multitier supply chain interactions beforehand in order to determine the potentially applicable management practices for a later stage of the project initiative. In this chapter, characteristics of buyer-sub-supplier relationships are analyzed and demonstrated in three industry cases. Furthermore, current sub-supplier management practices and structures are defined and categorized.

## 1 Different Ways of Interacting with Sub-suppliers

Engaging in sub-supplier management activities requires insights into the characteristics and dynamics of a firm's multitier supply chain interactions. These determine the potentially applicable management practices for a later stage of the project initiative.

### *1.1 Characteristics of Buyer-Sub-supplier Relationships*

Buyer-sub-supplier relationships can be characterized by various factors. The type of interaction in which a buying firm interacts with its sub-supplier is one of the main factors upon which to analyze its lower-tier relationships. Within the various interaction types, different forms of management activities from a buying firm's perspective are applied through the application of decedent sub-supplier management practices (Tachizawa and Wong 2014).

E. Altmayer (✉) · I. Schönwandt
Institute of Supply Chain Management, University of St. Gallen, St. Gallen, Switzerland
e-mail: elisabeth.altmayer@unisg.ch

© The Author(s), under exclusive license to Springer Nature Switzerland AG 2021 
W. Stoelzle, J. Burkhardt (eds.), *Sub-Supplier Management*, Contributions to Management Science, https://doi.org/10.1007/978-3-030-75575-1_2

## 1.2 Analyzing Buyer-Sub-supplier Relationships Step by Step

At first, an analysis and a description of buyer-supplier-sub-supplier relationship types are conducted. This analysis includes existent sub-supplier management activities and interaction types, as well as a detailed description of interaction types. A second step includes identification of factors determining buyer-supplier-sub-supplier relationship. These determining factors are referring to contextual variants leading to a specific buyer-sub-supplier interaction to be successful or unsuccessful from a buying company's perspective. Insight on these factors is crucial for future (re-)design and introduction of new interactive activities and practices.

In its smallest extent, a multitier supply chain consists of three actors, the buying company, the direct supplier, and the sub-supplier. This is also called a supply chain triad. The various interaction types within a triad can be categorized in eight different categories, whereas types one to five can be found frequently, and types six to eight are rather seldom, as they are usually a compromise solution for a problematic relationship within the triad (Hofstetter 2018) (Figs. 1 and 2).

For the evaluation of the various interaction types within a company's multitier supply chains, it is crucial not only to be aware of the most common types of interactions but also to further get an idea for the reasons (positively as well as negatively related) for the discovered structures. Based on this insight, within a later optimizing phase, several actions—best practices if you will—can be fitted.

Positively related factors lead to a specific interaction type. They are advantages that arise from the buying company through the application of this type of interaction. Negatively related reasons are determinants that keep the firm from engaging in an alternative interaction type.

Figure 3 provides an overview of typical, often discovered characteristics within supply chains as well as positively and negatively related reasons for the application of the various interaction types found in buying companies from diverse industries.

## 1.3 Recommendation: Analysis of Current Interaction with Sub-suppliers

The identification of factors determining firm-sub-supplier interactions follows a four-step analysis process (Fig. 4).

1. Identification of existing interaction types according to the typology introduced
2. Estimation of interaction type percentages based on supplier (relationship management) data within the firm
3. Evaluation of reasons for the current type of interaction to ensure potential benefits (positively related) as well as reasons for avoiding a type of interaction to prevent potential risks (negatively related)

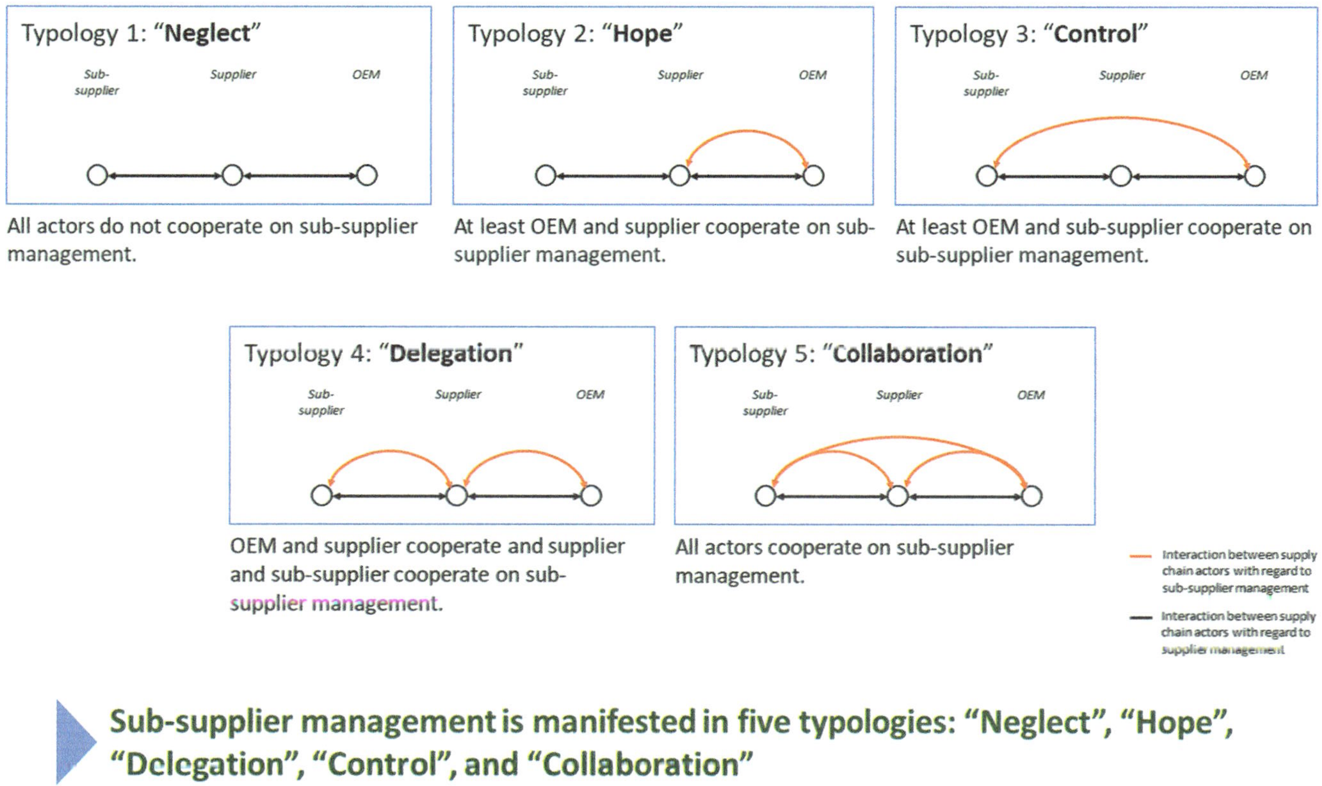


**Fig. 1** Delineation of sub-supplier management by five typologies. Source: Authors' own illustration

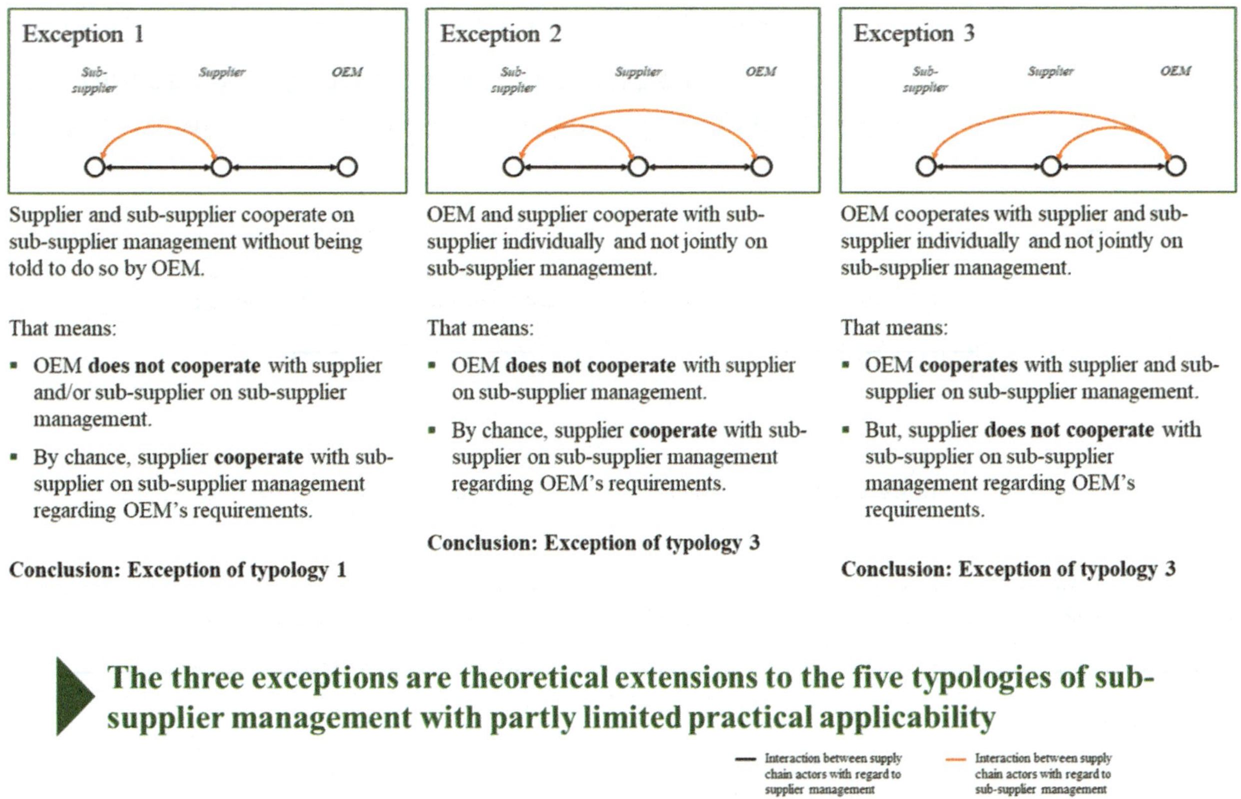


**Fig. 2** Three exceptions adding to the five typologies of sub-supplier management. Source: Authors' own illustration

| Type of interaction | | Characteristics | Positively related reasons* | Negatively related reasons* |
|---|---|---|---|---|
| **Competition** | 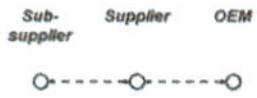 | ▪ Main type of interaction in business-as-usual situation | ▪ Used for tendering<br>▪ No management necessary, because of irrelevant supply chain / market buying is sufficient | ▪ Lack of long-term collaboration<br>▪ Lack of market transparency |
| **Certification** | 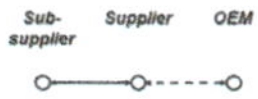 | ▪ In selected individual cases | ▪ Meet product-specific requirements<br>▪ Option for sub-supplier development<br>▪ High flexibility<br>▪ In selected cases, for traders | ▪ Lack of influence on direct supplier |
| **Delegation** | 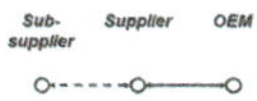 | ▪ Main type of interaction in business-as-usual situation<br>▪ Reactive sub-supplier management | ▪ Complexity reduction<br>▪ High degree of control, enabled through high degree of specification and declaration of conformity<br>▪ Balance of power of big sub-suppliers, enabled through cooperation with big direct suppliers with the ability to influence the sub-suppliers | ▪ Power relations, i.e. power potential of big sub-suppliers<br>▪ (Sub-)supplier unknown / no willingness to get to know<br>▪ No direct control if supplier pass on company's specific policies and requirements |
| **Commitment** | 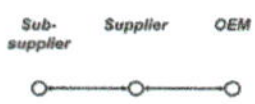 | ▪ For selected individual cases<br>▪ For trustful, long-term relationships | ▪ Personal contact to and resulting long-term relationship with producers / growers<br>▪ Fair pricing<br>▪ Role as main customer of direct supplier, improving supplier potential at sub-supplier level<br>▪ Request of commitment at supplier-level for sub-supplier control in terms of audits, supply of materials, etc. | ▪ Difficult to implement and maintain<br>▪ Time- and resource-consuming<br>▪ Increased responsibility, e.g. in case of deterioration of relationship, supply problems<br>▪ Critical concerning impact of suppliers |
| **Cooperation** | 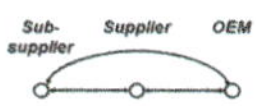 | ▪ For selected individual cases / critical supply chains<br>▪ For trustful, long-term relationships | ▪ Development of long-term relationships<br>▪ Support through consultation and fair pricing, with the intention of supporting sub-supplier independence, increasing (sub-) supplier motivation<br>▪ Existing relationship with sub-suppliers, e.g. through direct supply relationship in other aspects<br>▪ Explicit strive for cooperation, through joint development with suppliers and sub-suppliers<br>▪ Long-term commitment | ▪ Very time- and resource-consuming<br>▪ Requires proactive sub-supplier management<br>▪ Dependence on sub-supplier through type of relationship, i.e. compulsory sourcing independent of requirements<br>▪ Relationship problems between suppliers and sub-suppliers, e.g. through power differences |
| **Bypass** | 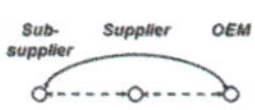 | ▪ Exceptional case: rarely found | ▪ n/a | ▪ n/a |
| **Parallel** | 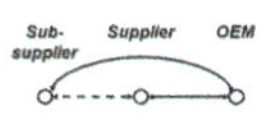 | ▪ Exceptional case: rarely found | ▪ Open communication | ▪ Different power relations<br>▪ Cultural differences |
| **Back-Door** | 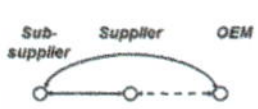 | ▪ Exceptional case: rarely found<br>▪ Option when working with large sub-suppliers with great power potential | ▪ Direct suppliers with lack of willingness to cooperate | ▪ High level of complexity |

**Fig. 3** Detailed description of interaction types. Source: Authors' own table

4. Summary of evaluation results regarding most influential factors determining the firms' sub-supplier interaction for future optimization phase of the management practices and processes

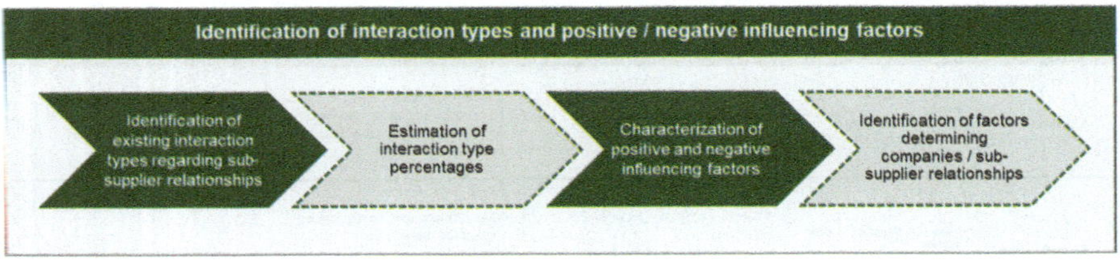


**Fig. 4** Four steps to analyze firm-sub-supplier interaction. Source: Authors' own illustration

## *1.4 Three Industry Cases: Analysis of Interaction Types and Buying Power as Major Determining Factors*

The following three case studies relating to the SFS Group, ThyssenKrupp AG, and former Weidenhammer Packaging Group were conducted in 2016 based on interviews with company representatives with insights into procurement and sales activities. The respective company background of that year is provided as an introduction to each case.

## *1.5 Case 1: SFS*

### 1.5.1 Background Information on the SFS Group

The SFS Group AG develops and manufactures precision-formed components and fastening solutions for various industries, e.g., automobile, high tech, aerospace, and construction. Automotive is the most important market for SFS, and the overarching division "Engineered Components" (also including business activities in aerospace, electrical and electronics, and special applications) generates revenues of about CHF 740 million. Furthermore, the company is organized in regions (Europe, North America, and Asia), each one with its distinct procurement and sales department and decentralized processes. The headquarters in Heerbrugg comprise about 1400 employees in a wide range of divisions (almost 8000 employee worldwide). SFS' suppliers range from producers of steel, oil, chemical products, tensile force parts, and various tools to service providers for heating and surface treatments as well as waste disposal and outfitters (SFS Group AG 2016) (Table 1).

Depending on the products, SFS is a tier 1 and tier 2 supplier, delivering to OEMs and system manufacturers, respectively. SFS experiences intense pressure in the automotive industry and increasingly stringent market conditions driven by OEM supply chain management practices. Otherwise, SFS practices an "open door culture" and rather informal relationships with the largest strategic partners. The predominant interaction type that characterizes SFS sub-supplier management is typology 4 "Delegation." SFS actively tries to develop strong ties to both buyers and suppliers. Additionally, it strongly opposes "Parallel" interaction types such as in

**Table 1** Supply chain perception of SFS distinguishing between buyers in automotive and hardware components

| The focal firm's perception towards | Buyers of automotive components (tier 1) | Buyers of hardware components (OEMs) | Suppliers |
|---|---|---|---|
| Direction of analysis | Downstream | Downstream | Upstream |
| 1st power position | Dependence | Dependence | Strength |
| Interaction | Direct | Direct | Direct |
| Management approaches | Close, innovation process, also going to OEM | A close, informal, innovation process | Intensive relationship building, company visits 2–3 times per year, involvement in the innovation process |
| 2nd power position | Strength but treated by the focal firm as inequality | Strength | Dependence |
| Interaction | Direct | Direct | Direct but in some cases also no interaction |
| Management approaches | Close, informal | Close, informal | Close, innovation process |

Source: Authors' own table

"Exception 3," in which OEMs cooperate with both the supplier and sub-supplier without the supplier and sub-supplier cooperating.

### 1.5.2 SFS' Supplier Relationships

SFS practices intensive relationship building. The benefits of maintaining close relationships outweigh the drawbacks from such dependences. From a global perspective, SFS operates strictly in three regions. Therefore, the raw materials for SFS in Europe are sourced only from European rolling and drawing mills, steelworks, and plastics granules producers. These suppliers are typically price-setters for the raw materials in this field. However, a considerable purchasing volume and the interchangeability of its suppliers provide SFS with a reasonably strong position in negotiations and enable to undertake innovation projects with suppliers. SFS primarily seeks to maintain long-lasting and close relationships with its suppliers because the learning effect significantly increases the quality of goods from suppliers. Derived from the high standards in the automobile industry, SFS conducts extensive supplier acquisition processes and maintains specific audit intervals with its 20+ strategic suppliers.

Additionally, SFS representatives visit its largest suppliers two to three times per year, which it uses to build relationships and coordinate innovation processes. The link towards its sub-suppliers, consisting of mining companies and coking coal producers, is characterized by significant distance, which limits its ability to transmit standards and requirements. Since SFS strictly purchases from defined European regions, the market standards are rather homogenous. Therefore, SFS in Europe is protected against social and environmental compliance issues that could arise when purchasing from outside markets. Furthermore, relative bargaining strength is critically dependent on the point of view and the partner's organizational structure. Therefore, the specific contracting party differentiates between a position of power or dependency for SFS.

### 1.5.3 SFS' Buyer Relationships

Despite being in a position of dependence as a supplier, SFS draws supporting strength from its diverse setup as well as intensive and long-term focused relationship building. SFS supplies four different sectors at similar shares of revenue contribution and thereby relieves significant market pressure through diversification. Primarily being a tier 2 supplier to the automobile industry, SFS' size and diversity provide flexibility and security from extortion through buyers. Being able to produce at the same quality worldwide makes the company particularly attractive for the automotive sector. Nonetheless, specific automotive market characteristics, such as e-auctions and "pay-to-play" practices, present significant hurdles in competing for orders of commoditized products (see Fig. 5).

To mitigate purely price-focused negotiations, SFS practices relationship management on all levels of the tendering process. This complexity and the common practice of job rotation in buyers' procurement departments prevent relationships to develop and maintain a competitive environment and low commodity prices. Nonetheless, despite rotations, establishing connections at least increases the sensitivity on the buyer. For example, SFS experienced higher chances of receiving early warnings about potential competing offers in the past.

Outside the automotive sector, relationship building is equally essential to SFS. Maintaining long-lasting customer relationships is potentially easier in the hardware components sector. The competition is also intense in this field, and suppliers become increasingly exchangeable. Being a renowned automotive supplier, on the one hand, benefits SFS with a reputation for high quality but on the other also harms competitiveness through higher prices resulting from maintaining higher standards. SFS aims to be involved as early as possible by contributing to design and development of new parts. This approach builds moral bonds with customers and can win first order contracts, although SFS is asking for prices slightly above the competitive market price. Being known for reliability and financial strength, SFS becomes more involved with its customers by taking on responsibility through managing the supply of entire assembly lines.

Meeting compliance standards is not an issue for SFS within the European market. Additionally, SFS also takes into consideration special compliance requests and implements them depending on the customer's purchasing volume and similar demands by other customers.

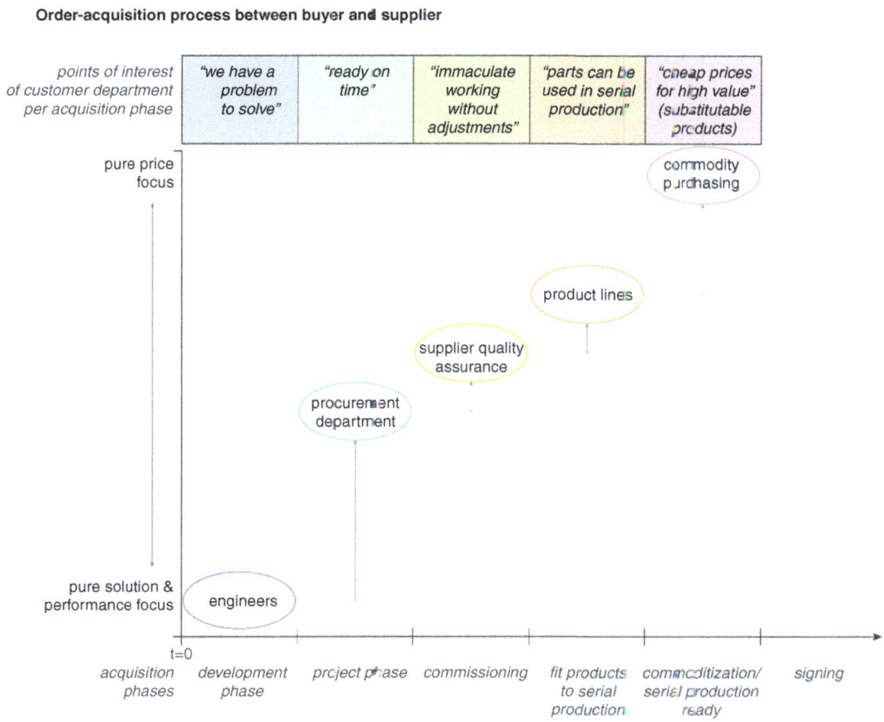


**Fig. 5** Order acquisition process between buyer and supplier. Source: Authors' own illustration

## 1.6 *Case 2: ThyssenKrupp Presta Steering*

### 1.6.1 Background Information on ThyssenKrupp Presta Steering

The ThyssenKrupp Presta AG Presta Steering is part of the ThyssenKrupp affiliated group, located in the Components Technology division. TK Presta is a tier 1 supplier to the automotive industry and has four groups of products relating to automotive power trains and steering with a combined annual turnover of about CHF 1.8 billion. Due to expensive logistics as a system manufacturer, TK Presta has 16 factories worldwide to enable assembly on-site close to the OEMs. It is globally set up in a matrix structure of Operation Units and Customer Business Units (CBUs), who's regional representatives of project leaders and cluster managers manage their own procurement process. In general, Presta procures mainly electronic parts, sheet metal, castings, and rubber parts as its raw materials, which are then formed and itemized by Presta. It is very focused on a market with only few potential customers, the premium automotive brands, and in turn offers a medium range of different products and presents innovation (ThyssenKrupp AG 2015) (Table 2).

ThyssenKrupp Presta manages order acquisitions independently from the ThyssenKrupp Group and thus typically finds themselves in a position of

**Table 2** Supply chain perception of ThyssenKrupp Presta Steering

| The focal firm's perception towards | Buyers (OEMs) | Suppliers (tier 2) |
|---|---|---|
| Direction of analysis | Downstream | Upstream |
| 1st power position | Dependence | Strength |
| Interaction types | Direct | Direct |
| Management approaches | Mostly in application and development phase, rather rudimentary | Mostly in the acquisition phase, company visits of strategic suppliers and in case of problems, rather rudimentary |
| 2nd power position | – | – |

Source: Authors' own table

dependence on buyers. It operates worldwide, and its supply network position is influenced by its buyers, the competition, regulators, and sector-specific standards and requirements. TK Presta's supply chain interactions are predominantly characterized by typology 1 "Neglect" and "Competition." In some cases, TK Presta is being "bypassed" by OEMs, who order sub-suppliers to deliver parts to TK Presta for assembly, representing an extended version of interaction type "Exception 3." The reach of OEMs can extend to TK Presta (tier 2) and even its suppliers in exceptional cases of major recalls ("Exception 3"/"Parallel interaction").

### 1.6.2 TK Presta's Supplier Relationships

Supplier acquisition at TK Presta is a fact-based, structured process summarized as "front-loading," aiming to evaluate and reduce the risks of future long-term production contracts. Various steps are taken to ascertain the most capable and secure suppliers before going into sample testing and conducting a purchasing assessment, including compliance issues and responsibilities, which lead to finalizing the contract. Over the period of the contract, TK Presta requires suppliers to qualify their products yearly. Personal visits are conducted only with new suppliers or if problems occurred in the past. In a few cases, an OEM autonomously arranges a sub-supplier to deliver parts.

Furthermore, TK Presta issues compliance requests following the requests from OEMs and the own standards from the ThyssenKrupp group mainly through contracts. However, often, TK Presta is not able to verify suppliers' compliance, primarily with Asian suppliers.

### 1.6.3 TK Presta's Buyer Relationships

Due to the competitive market, commoditization levels are high, and TK Presta receives intense pressure from buyers, the tier 1 systems manufacturers. As a result, supply chain relationships show competitive behavior and increasing distrust, secrecy, obscurity, and distance between the partners. TK Presta tries to mitigate such pressures with innovation but still finds themselves in a position of dependence.

## 1.7 *Case 3: Weidenhammer*

### 1.7.1 Background Information on Weidenhammer Packaging Group

The Weidenhammer Packaging Group is a tier 1 supplier and Europe's leading provider of composite cans and drums for the food and consumer industry. Customers include affiliated groups like Nestlé, Procter & Gamble, Unilever, Kellogg, as well as tobacco producers. Weidenhammer, which has a long history as a family business, has been acquired by the Sonoco Products Company (Sonoco) from South Carolina in the USA in October 2014 and is currently undergoing an integration process. Weidenhammer reported an annual turnover of about EUR 300 million, whereas Sonoco would have about USD5 billion annual turnover. Weidenhammer's packaging solutions are very specific but can be used in different sectors, especially the food and tobacco industry, and thus are potentially useful to a wide range of companies (Table 3).

Weidenhammer's supply chain strategy focuses on engaging all suppliers, including smaller ones, as well as its buyers to create open and trusting relationships, foster

**Table 3** Supply chain perception of Weidenhammer Packaging Group

| The focal firm's perception towards | Buyers (OEM) | Suppliers (tier 2) |
|---|---|---|
| Direction of analysis | Downstream | Upstream |
| 1st power position | Dependence/equal | Strength/equal |
| Interaction types | Direct | Direct, up to tier 4 |
| Management approaches | Relationships built on trust and transparency | Relationships built on trust and transparency, close collaboration, efficiency initiatives, personal relationship building, joint sourcing of materials with all levels of suppliers |
| 2nd power position | – | Equal/strength (tier n) |
| Interaction types | – | Direct, indirect |
| Management approaches | – | A relationship built on trust and transparency |

Source: Authors' own table

a holistic understanding of the partners, and collaborate on efficiency improvements wherever possible. As a packaging supplier for the food and luxury goods industries, Weidenhammer supplies some of the largest companies in the sector. On the opposite, it sources its raw materials from a variety of smaller sub-suppliers. The main ingredients are paper, plastic, and aluminum. Thus, Weidenhammer generally experiences a dependence on buyers and strength over suppliers. However, due to a combination of the specificity of its packaging products, which are highly associated by consumers with the products they are containing, and little competition in its field, Weidenhammer can engage in open discussions with its buyers. Simultaneously, it does not exploit its position over suppliers but instead encourages them to optimize the supply chain as a whole. Between its buyers and suppliers, Weidenhammer is the only link. The rest of the supply chain's interactions are characterized by typology 5 "Collaboration." Additionally, it immediately prevents attempts of its customers to autonomously organize sub-suppliers as in the "Bypass"/ "Exception 3" scenarios, which could threaten its supply chain's trust and efficiency.

### 1.7.2 Weidenhammer's Supplier Relationships

Upstream, Weidenhammer has convinced partners of the benefits of an "open book policy" and even engages in its suppliers' and sub-suppliers' procurement processes. Profit-sharing arrangements and fair price setting are an integral part of the regular meetings with suppliers. Efficiency benefits from supply chain improvements are shared with its partners. This custom strengthens Weidenhammer's position with buyers. In raw material procurement, Weidenhammer represents a collective of small, yet similar producers with the same resource needs. This collective purchasing strategy allows to source materials in larger quantities and at lower prices.

### 1.7.3 Weidenhammer's Buyer Relationships

The procurement department frequently joins sales negotiations with customers. Sharing supply chain characteristics with the customers enables them to reflect on their own decisions concerning the total efficiency of the supply chain. The customers' buying decisions can significantly impact the total cost of production. Allowing the customers to see the big picture can mitigate adverse buying behavior, which would lead to efficiency losses of the supply chain. Weidenhammer's customers, therefore, value its extensive supply chain engagement for an improved time-to-market and more reliable forecasting ability.

Nonetheless, maintaining an equal level of trust with its customers is challenging. Generally, Weidenhammer complies with sustainability standards from customers. However, additional requests are also considered. When such requests demand significant changes, decisions are efficiency-based.

## 2 Sub-supplier Management Practices

Within the interaction types of a firm and its supply chain triad, specific management practices take place embedded in corporate structures at the buying firms. To be able to later extend or introduce sub-supplier management practices, identification, description, and evaluation of established sub-supplier management practices and structures in sub-supplier management is crucial.

Although often not aware of the fact, most buying companies already have established sub-supplier management practice in place. However, these usually are unrecognized as such as well as take place uncoordinatedly. In any buying firm, you can find a specific set of sub-supplier management practices, namely, contractual obligations of direct suppliers to delegate requirements to sub-suppliers, the requirement of certifications of purchased goods, and singular direct involvement with specific sub-suppliers in development programs.

Since some sub-supplier management practices are only applied in critical situations when issues within the lower-tier supply chains have become apparent, one can differentiate between practices used in day-to-day business and those practices applied as a reaction to an incident. Depending on the particular contextual situation and applied practice, the interaction type within a specific supply chain triad can switch in cases of critical events, respectively, and business as usual (Fig. 6).

When describing supply chain objectives impacted by sub-suppliers, again a processual multistep analysis is recommended. Starting with a project-centric collection of objectives to be addressed with a sub-supplier management project, furthermore, additional potential general objectives for the firm are collected to ensure non-conflicts. These objectives then are specified and prioritized based on budget and time constraints, resulting in a (list of) focused objectives for a sub-supplier management project initiative.

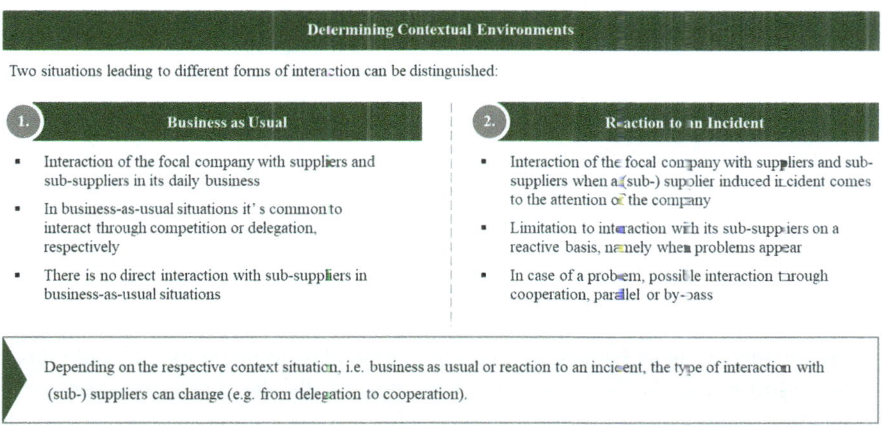


**Fig. 6** Identification of factors determining OEM/sub-supplier relationships. Source: Authors' own illustration

Besides the collection of practices and corporate structures used to manage sub-suppliers, their evaluation of positive and negative reasons for investigated findings has to take place to provide a base for future improvements in sub-supplier management. Furthermore, it is of interest to evaluate existing practices within a firm upon their effectiveness and reach. Effectiveness thereby refers to the degree upon which the intended objectives and results are achieved through a sub-supplier management practice as perceived by the buying company. The reach of a sub-supplier management practice describes how far upstream the practice can make its impact within the lower tiers of the supply chain.

## 2.1 Three Main Categories of Sub-supplier Management Practices

In general, there are three groups of sub-supplier management practices (Hofstetter 2018):

1. Management practices
2. Selection practices
3. Additional practices

The following illustration provides an extensive list of the practices of all three categories (Figs. 7 and 8).

Further analyzation of most common sub-supplier management practices within a company contains a detailed description of the practices as well as the surrounding corporate structure.

## 2.2 The Most Common Sub-supplier Management Practices in Place

The following sub-supplier management practices can be frequently identified even in companies that don't have an explicit sub-supplier management in place. Usually, they are performed by the strategic purchasing department:

- Develop suppliers and sub-suppliers: This practice encompasses financial investments in and the development of sub-suppliers, know-how transfer, networking, investments in cooperation or service provider, incentive systems, companies giving advice, financial support and know-how, development of a suitable product solution together with sub-suppliers, and finally the typical reaction to an incident approach.
- Sub-supplier performance dashboard to detect risks on the sub-supplier-level early on: The aim is to declare commitment with distributors to disclose

*(1) Management practices*

1. Establish a trustful relationship with suppliers
2. Establish a trustful relationship with sub-suppliers
3. Clearly debate requirements (must be measureable) and their achievements in periodic discussions
4. Structurally invite suppliers and sub-suppliers feedback / statement (e.g., technical feasibility)
5. Demonstrate the relevance and benefits of compliance with requirements
6. Motivate (oblige) suppliers and sub-suppliers to get certified (e.g., ISO 9000 in automotive industry as a basic requirements, regulatory, technical requirements)
7. Confront suppliers and sub-suppliers with performance gaps
8. Discuss performance gaps with regard to consequences
9. Develop suppliers and sub-suppliers
10. Acquisition of suppliers
11. Acquisition of sub-suppliers
12. Request supply chain transparency
13. Escalate up to senior management in the corporation
14. Sustainability audits / voluntary sustainability initiatives (VSI)
15. Cooperation with further customers of sub-suppliers / suppliers (i.e., increase buying power)
16. 2nd party audits (i.e., audit is conducted by OEM) / inspection
17. Define role of suppliers (i.e., value add)
18. Communicate business case for sub-suppliers
19. Communicate role / impact of sub-suppliers to OEM (TQM)
20. Integrate price negotiations, supplier selection, and supplier / sub-supplier development (i.e., one clear strategy to sub-suppliers)
21. Help suppliers in understanding the sub-suppliers markets
22. Establish a sub-supplier management process together with suppliers
23. Explain the suppliers the benefit of sub-supplier management
24. Sub-supplier performance dashboard to early detect risks on sub-supplier-level

**Fig. 7** Sub-supplier management practices. Source: Authors' own illustration

| *(2) Selection practices* | *(3) Additional practices* |
|---|---|
| 1. Switch suppliers | 1. Participate in industry initiatives (i.e., pooling demands with other firms; e.g., sourcing cooperation, round tables) |
| 2. Switch sub-suppliers | 2. Get involved in sourcing region / involve local internal parties |
| 3. Motivate (oblige) suppliers to switch sub-suppliers | 3. Ignite and fuel a debate about an issue (i.e., internally) |
| 4. Predefine sub-suppliers and advise suppliers to buy from these preselected sub-suppliers | 4. Ignite and fuel a debate about an issue (i.e., public) |
| 5. Use transparency as criterion for supplier selection | 5. Set up different collaborations on technical and commercial base (i.e., commercial collaboration between OEM and sub-supplier and technical collaboration between supplier and sub-supplier) |
| 6. Source certified products only | 6. Get external support |
| 7. Source from certified suppliers only | |
| 8. Establish second source | |
| 9. Motivate suppliers to establish second source (i.e., sub-supplier) | |
| 10. Prefer "alikes" when choosing new suppliers (e.g., cooperation must make sense for both actors) | |
| 11. Extend selection criteria (supplier evaluation process) | |
| 12. Predefine sub-suppliers | |

**Fig. 8** Sub-supplier selection and additional practices. Source: Authors' own illustration

production sites and guarantee quality status. It can also help to identify risks in sub-supplier chains.
- Set up different collaborations on a technical and commercial base: An analysis of cooperation for specific products to minimize risks, gain know-how, and support innovative suppliers. It is managed through tendering. Such a collaboration is also possible through the creation of a procurement network with further customers of (the same) sub-suppliers.
- Explain the benefit of sub-supplier management to suppliers: This is done through workshops with (sub-)suppliers to align objectives. The buying firm communicates existing standards towards suppliers who then commit to observe and control observations for sub-suppliers. This incentive system leads to commitment, as the company demands quality requirements from suppliers that also improve the supplier's quality.
- Request supply chain transparency: Most sub-suppliers are unknown, so there is a need for identification as well as for analysis of procurement risks and cost-saving potentials.
- Establish a sub-supplier management process together with suppliers: Taking early-stage decisions regarding future collaboration. The buying company can implement this practice through collaboration in committees.
- Predefine sub-suppliers and advise suppliers to buy from these preselected sub-suppliers: This enables a selection of direct suppliers via sub-suppliers.
- Switch (sub-)supplier: In case of problems, for example, with quality, sub-supplier can be switched. Usually, a complaint system is established. After a defined number of complaints, a conversation takes place. To ensure quality, an audit with predefined measures for improvement is conducted.
- Establish a trustful relationship with (sub-)suppliers: To accomplish this, the buying company should communicate transparently with all relevant supply chains actors, share relevant data and information proactively, or engage in joint development activities (sub-)suppliers (Table 4).

## 2.3 *Analysis of Practices: Identify Success Factors*

For a further breakdown of existing sub-supplier management practices, it is advisable to include the type of interaction, positive influencing, and negative influencing factors for each of the sub-supplier management practices collected. These influencing factors function as critical success factors for the desired outcome of the applied practice (Fig. 9).

Exemplary analysis results of a few of the most common sub-supplier management practices are illustrated within the Table 5.

**Table 4** Description of the most common sub-supplier management practices

| Practice | Description |
|---|---|
| Develop suppliers and sub-suppliers | – Financial investments in sub-suppliers, development of sub-suppliers, know-how transfer (e.g., through educational courses), networking (e.g., in roundtables)<br>– Investments in cooperation/service provider<br>– Incentive system: Company demands quality requirements from suppliers that also improve the supplier's quality; leads to commitment<br>– The buying company gives advice, financial support, know-how<br>– Development of suitable product solutions together with sup-suppliers<br>– Common: Reaction to an incident |
| Sub-supplier performance dashboard to early detect risks on sub-supplier-level | – Declaration of commitment with distributors to disclose production sites and guarantee the quality status<br>– Identify risks in sub-supplier chains |
| Set up different collaborations on technical and commercial base | – Analysis of cooperation for specific products to minimize risks, gain know-how, and support innovative suppliers<br>– Manage the competitive situation regarding procurement through tendering<br>– Procurement network with further customers of sub-suppliers |
| Explain the suppliers the benefit of sub-supplier management | – Workshops with (sub-)suppliers to align objectives<br>– Communicate existing standards towards the supplier<br>– The direct supplier commits to observe guidelines and standards, as well as controls observation for sub-suppliers<br>– Incentive system: company demands quality requirements from suppliers that also improve the supplier's quality; leads to commitment |
| Request supply chain transparency | – If the majority of the sub-suppliers unknown: the need for identification as well as analysis of procurement risks and cost-saving potentials<br>– Common: Reaction to an incident |
| Establish a sub-supplier management process together with suppliers | – Take early-stage decisions regarding future collaboration<br>– Collaboration in committees<br>– The requirement of particular standards from sub-suppliers |
| Predefine sub-suppliers and advise suppliers to buy from these preselected sub-suppliers | – Selection of direct suppliers via sub-suppliers<br>– Mainly preferred suppliers of the buying company are predefined |
| Switch (sub-)supplier | – In case of problems (e.g., quality), sub-supplier can be switched<br>– Complaint system: there is a conversation after |

(continued)

**Table 4** (continued)

| Practice | Description |
|---|---|
| | a defined number of complaints (personal, at the supplier's location)<br>– Quality: audit with predefined measures for improvement<br>– Attempt to develop a new system due to a supplier switch |
| Establish a trustful relationship with (sub-) suppliers | – Communicate transparency<br>– Build active trust due to communication measure<br>– Joint development with single-sourced direct suppliers<br>– The higher specification, the more input is given to the supplier or sub-supplier (e.g., regarding design) |

Source: Authors' own table

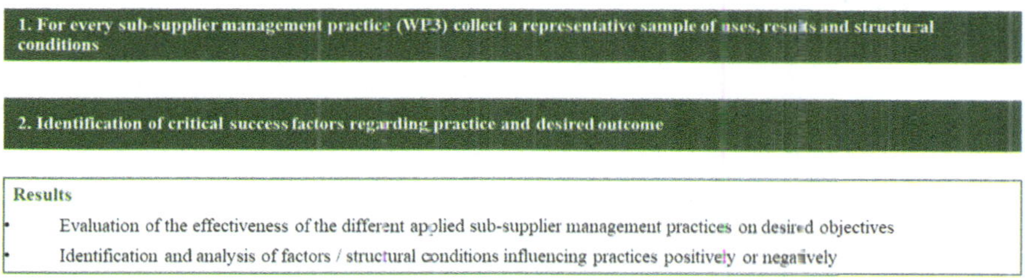


**Fig. 9** Analysis of current sub-supplier management effectiveness and reach. Source: Authors' own illustration

## 2.4 *Existing Sub-supplier Management Practices: How Effective Are They and Do They Reach the Lower Tiers?*

When analyzing already applied sub-supplier management processes, it essential to determine whether these are effective in regard to achieving the desired objectives. In the context of sub-supplier management practices, effectiveness is often a question of whether the process even reaches the sub-supplier, mainly if practices are applied within a delegation interaction via direct suppliers. Therefore, sub-supplier practices should be analyzed upon their reach as to how far they are affecting the lower-tier sub-supplier's behavior.

**Table 5** Exemplary analysis of sub-supplier management practices upon critical success factors

| Practice | Responsibility | Interaction | Positive influencing factors | Negative influencing factors |
|---|---|---|---|---|
| Explain the suppliers the benefit of sub-supplier management/strategy alignment | (Strategic) procurement/ quality | Cooperation/ delegation/ commitment | – Long-term strategy alignment<br>– Commitment<br>– Reduction of monitoring costs<br>– Low institutional/federal pressure<br>– Common basic understanding of both parties: Kaizen approach is reasonable | – Transfer of guidelines and requirements to next-tier supplier complicated<br>– Price pressure |
| Sub-supplier performance dashboard to early detect risks on sub-supplier-level | (Strategic) procurement/ quality | Certification/ delegation/ cooperation | – Communication with the involved partners<br>– Reduction of monitoring costs<br>– Trust and long-term relationship with the supplier<br>– A supplier must have a good relationship with his suppliers | – One-third of all dealers do not provide relevant information<br>– Dealers: lack of understanding regarding the duty of care<br>– Information sharing |
| Establish a sub-supplier management process together with suppliers | (Strategic) procurement | Parallel/ bypass/ delegation | – Communication with the supplier and sub-supplier<br>– Shared understanding between all three parties about requirements | – Problems with the competition commission<br>– Regulatory adjustments difficulties between partners<br>– Feasibility along the supply chain with all the partners<br>– A shared understanding of responsibility for the development of the sub-supplier<br>– Willingness to spent time/ resources on the development of sub-suppliers<br>– Management support |
| Establish a sub-supplier | (Strategic) procurement | | – Communication with the supplier | – Problems with the competition |

(continued)

**Table 5** (continued)

| Practice | Responsibility | Interaction | Positive influencing factors | Negative influencing factors |
|---|---|---|---|---|
| management process together with suppliers | | Parallel/ bypass/ delegation | and sub-supplier – Shared understanding between all three parties about requirements | commission – Regulatory adjustments difficulties between partners – Feasibility along the supply chain with all the partners – A shared understanding of responsibility for the development of the sub-supplier – Willingness to spent time/ resources on the development of sub-suppliers – Management support |

Source: Authors' own table

## *2.5 Case: Evaluation of the Delegation Practice in the Cacao Supply Chain upon Effectiveness and Reach*

### 2.5.1 Background

For chocolate manufacturers, sub-suppliers have been a long-standing challenge. Most of the world's cacao grows in West Africa on the Ivory Coast (around 70 % of the worldwide production). Other growing regions are in Middle and South America, as well as South Asia. In general, the growing areas are third-world countries, which in the past caused consumer's concern about the social standards under which cacao farmers work and get paid. This customer concern requires chocolate manufacturers to guarantee fair working and paying conditions through monitoring their supply chains through certificates and label organizations (Fig. 10).

Since the worldwide demand for cacao is increasing the production, chocolate manufacturers started active development programs with cacao farmers to ensure cacao supply. Through those programs, the cacao-buying firms invest heavily in the regions, for example, through developing the infrastructure or building schools. Additionally, they directly educate the farmers on efficient farming and growing of the plants. However, investing directly in these sub-suppliers often causes the issue that despite the efforts, farmers do not sell their harvest to the chocolate manufacturers that invested in them but to the highest bidder on the world market. Therefore, achievement of sub-supplier loyalty—thus prevention of so-called side-selling—is

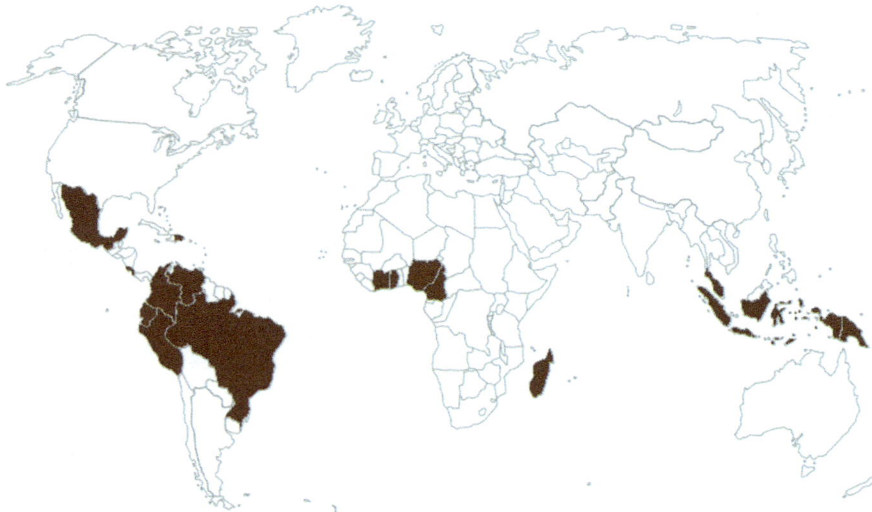

**Fig. 10** Cacao growth regions. Source: Authors' own illustration

one of the main objectives that cacao-buying companies are focusing on in their sub-supplier management efforts.

### 2.5.2 Case Explanation

The following case analyzes a chocolate manufacturer's supply chain and the applied sub-supplier management practices and effectiveness and reach in regard to achieving sub-supplier loyalty.

The buying company is one of Europe's largest chocolate producing firms, which buys cacao via a trading company, which is supplied by its local franchise holders on the Ivory Coast, who buy from a purchasing clerk, who again buys the cacao directly from several local farmers.

The buying chocolate manufacturer applies a delegation sub-supplier management practice via the trading company. The buyer engages in a long-term contract (4 years) with the trading company guaranteeing purchasing volumes and premium payment for engagement with their sub-suppliers. In return, the trading company has to ensure supply volumes by increasing sub-supplier loyalty. For this purpose, the trading company initiated a sustainability program that guarantees increased share for all farmers selling to this trader. The local franchise holders have a contract with the purchasing clerk, while there is a non-contractual gentlemen's agreement between the clerk and the local farmers.

Analysis of effectiveness and reach of the chocolate manufacturer's delegation approach shows that although loyalty between each single supply chain tier is high, the overall loyalty of farmers to sell into this supply chain is not optimal yet. Around 30% of the farmers' cacao is sold to other traders as a reaction to better prices offered from competitors or due to risk diversification (Fig. 11).

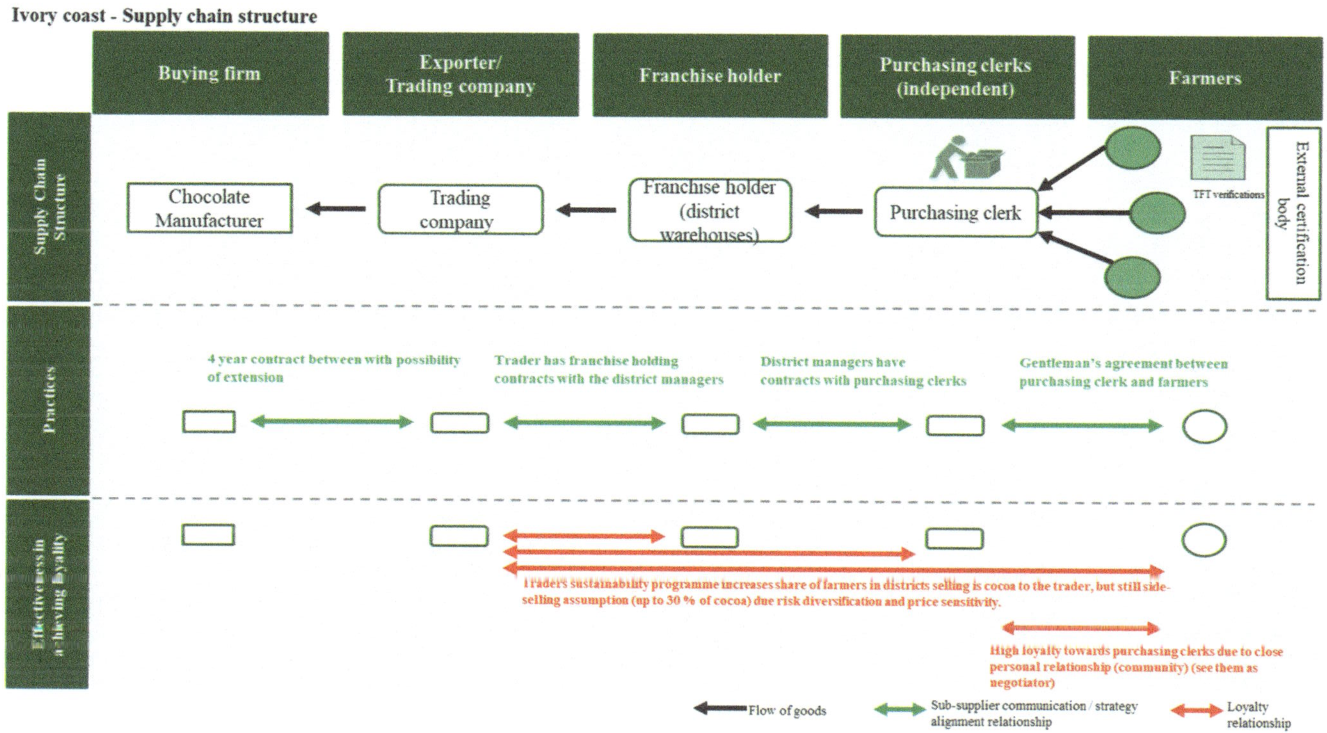


**Fig. 11** Effectiveness and reach of delegation practice in a cacao supply chain. Source: Authors' own illustration

## References

Hofstetter JS (2018) Extending management upstream in supply chains beyond direct suppliers. IEEE Eng Manag Rev 46:106–116

Tachizawa EM, Wong CY (2014) Towards a theory of multi-tier sustainable supply chains: a systematic literature review. Supply Chain Manag 19(5/6):643–663. https://doi.org/10.1108/SCM-02-2014-0070

# Introducing the Sub-supplier Management Framework

**Elisabeth Altmayer and Alissa Schwarz**

**Abstract** After an analysis of current challenges, objectives, structure, and activities in sub-supplier magnet upon their effectiveness and reach, new sub-supplier management activities can be planned, designed, and implemented. In this chapter, a process framework for sub-supplier management addressing various sub-supplier management objectives is introduced. The referential processes are considering variants for different interaction types and are applicable under consideration of multiple context factor variants. The practices should be suitable for integration within existing supplier management processes or on a project basis. The usage of the framework is demonstrated on the case of the Swiss pharmaceutical company Weleda.

## 1 Current Sub-supplier Management Structures and Practices

After an analysis of current challenges, objectives, structure, and activities in sub-supplier magnet upon their effectiveness and reach, new sub-supplier management activities can be planned, designed, and implemented. The following process framework for sub-supplier management categorizes and structures exemplary, generic processes addressing various sub-supplier management objectives. The referential processes are considering variants for different interaction types and are applicable under consideration of multiple context factor variants. The practices should be suitable for integration within existing supplier management processes or on a project basis (Fig. 1).

The sub-supplier management process framework is considering several levels of processes in three main categories: out-sub-supplier management, in-sub-supplier management, and in-sub-supplier dissolution management (Hofstetter 2018).

E. Altmayer (✉) · A. Schwarz
Institute of Supply Chain Management, University of St. Gallen, St. Gallen, Switzerland
e-mail: elisabeth.altmayer@unisg.ch

© The Author(s), under exclusive license to Springer Nature Switzerland AG 2021 
W. Stoelzle, J. Burkhardt (eds.), *Sub-Supplier Management*, Contributions to Management Science, https://doi.org/10.1007/978-3-030-75575-1_3

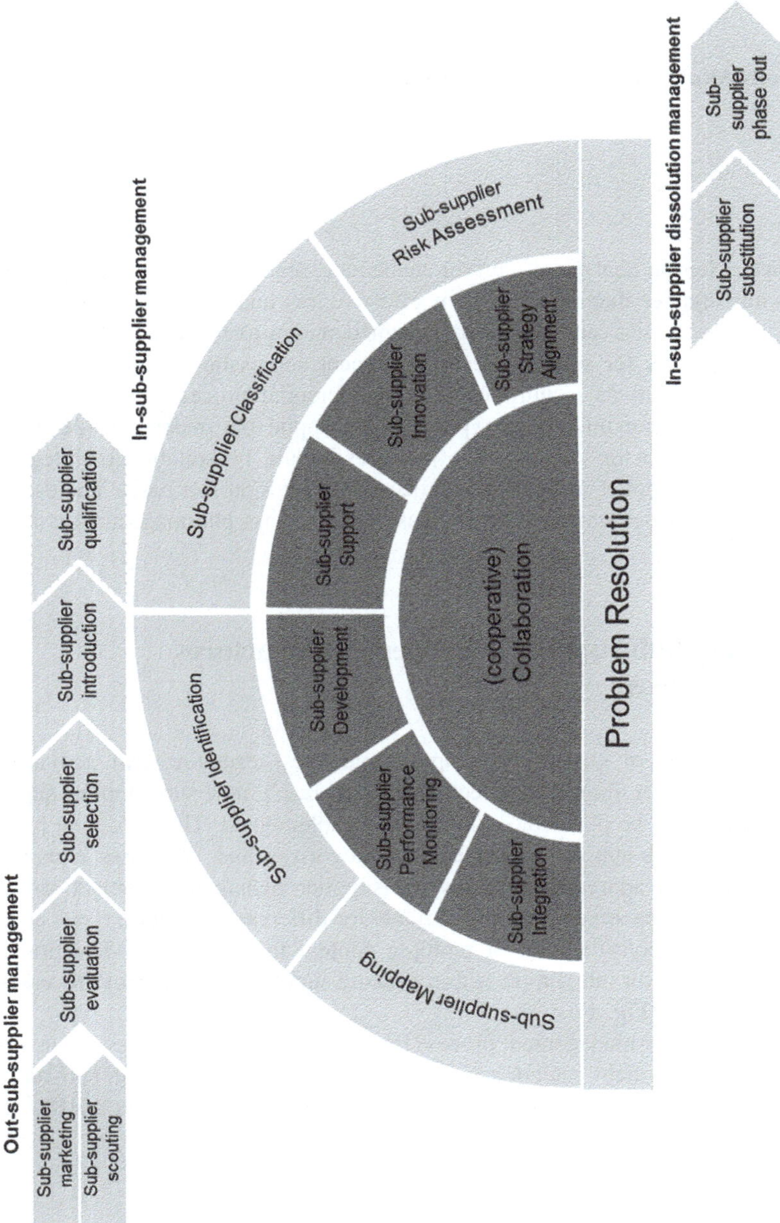


**Fig. 1** Sub-supplier management process framework. Source: Authors' own illustration

## *1.1 Out-Sub-supplier Management Process*

Out-sub-supplier management is combining several management processes revolving around integration of new sub-suppliers within a company's supply chain. The process flow starts with sub-supplier marketing and scouting, then sub-supplier evaluation, sub-supplier selection, sub-supplier introduction, and finally sub-supplier qualification:

- Sub-supplier marketing and scouting: Attracting sub-suppliers outside the supply chain, potentially through B2B marketing measures
- Sub-supplier evaluation and selection: Assessing sub-suppliers outside the supply chain and their performance, e.g., through evaluating their operational performance, financial performance, or reputation
- Sub-supplier introduction and qualification: Communication of Code of Conducts, company strategy, and the company requirements, e.g., through pre-scanning or questionnaires

## *1.2 In-Sub-supplier Dissolution Management Process*

In-sub-supplier dissolution management covers the issues that arise when a company wants to remove one of its sub-suppliers from its supply chain(s) It consists of the management processes sub-supplier substitution and sub-supplier phaseout:

- Sub-supplier substitution: Replacing the existing sub-supplier with a new sub-supplier, potentially involving out-sub-supplier management processes or sub-supplier identification
- Sub-supplier phase-out: Terminating any direct relationship with a sub-supplier (if existing) and removing the sub-supplier from the supply chain

In-sub-supplier management aims at addressing challenges and objectives with sub-suppliers that are actual actors within a company's supply chain. The inner process framework contains various sub-supplier management processes aiming at different implementation objectives:

- Operative collaboration: Describing sourcing and procurement activities
- Problem resolution: In a business-as-usual situation or when reacting to a sub-supplier-induced incident; necessary for going concern
- Sub-supplier classification: Analyzing OEM-supplier-sub-supplier relationship and sub-supplier characteristics
- Sub-supplier development: Supporting sub-suppliers through relationship management, partnering/cooperation, or investments in sub-supplier capacity, e.g., through training or workshops, which are aimed at the improvement of sub-supplier performance

- Sub-supplier financial support: Supporting a sub-supplier through reduction of economic pressure, lengthening of payment terms, sharing of risk, and investment
- Sub-supplier identification: Identifying specific sub-suppliers as part of the supply chain (with the name of company) and collection of business-related information within the supply chain
- Sub-supplier innovation: Joint sharing of information, technology, and expertise to exploit the capabilities of sub-suppliers
- Sub-supplier integration: Integration of sub-supplier activities/responsibilities into company activities, e.g., components manufacturing, system design, or collaborative platform development
- Sub-supplier performance monitoring: Monitoring through sub-supplier self-assessment and audits conducted by the focal company or supplier
- Sub-supplier procurement support: Ensure sub-supplier has certifications, geographic reach, and operational scalability (this might involve transaction costs)
- Sub-supplier risk assessment: Identification and evaluation of risky sub-suppliers through, e.g., the evaluation of legal compliance and social and ethical responsibility
- Sub-supplier strategy alignment: Alignment of the sub-supplier's objectives with those of the OEM, which results in an increase of transparency and communication of the company strategy
- Supply chain mapping: Aims at the identification of the overall structure of, the modes of collaboration used by, and the relevance of specific levels in the supply chain

In the context of a project initiative in sub-supplier management, it is advisable to focus on few sub-supplier management reference processes to implement and adjust them to best address the firm's challenges and objectives while keeping close to already existing process and structures.

## 2 Customization of the Future Sub-supplier Management Process Framework for the Implementation in Your Company

For an adaption of selected sub-supplier management reference processes into the firm internal process landscape, a four-step project approach is recommended. After the selection of fitting sub-supplier management processes according to the previous chapter, next process outputs, outcomes, and benefits for selected sub-supplier management processes are defined. First, the desired output based on specific sub-supplier management objectives is defined. Building upon these results, the outcome for the company, in general, is determined. Next, existing as well as new KPIs and ERP performance data is used to measure the respective objectives. Finally, an interactive approach is used to define inputs and the corresponding

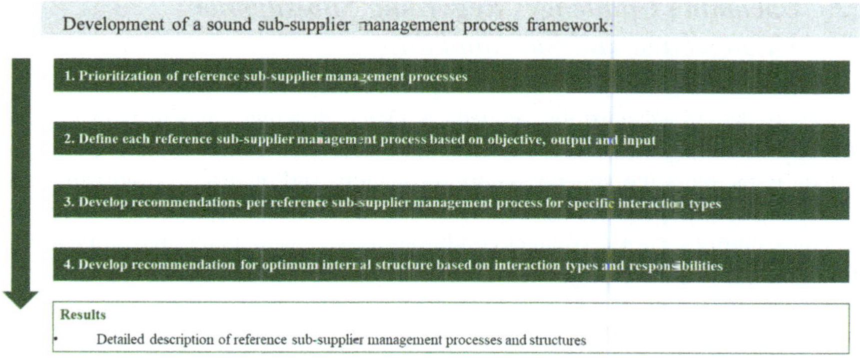


**Fig. 2** Definition of a customized sub-supplier management process framework, referential processes, and optimum structures. Source: Authors' own illustration

**Fig. 3** Weleda logo. Source: Internal Weleda brand logo

process elements. Examples of detailed processes are enclosed in the following chapter of this book (Fig. 2).

# 3 Case: Summarizing the Approach from Chapters 1 to 3 in an Example: Weleda (Fig. 3)

## *3.1 Background*

Weleda as a producer of natural organic cosmetics and anthroposophic pharmaceuticals has a diverse variety of suppliers and sub-suppliers, sourcing natural raw materials from fresh plants and drugs to fatty and essential oils as well as natural-based chemicals.

## 3.2 Upcoming Challenges Regarding Sub-supplier Management and Sustainability

Due to its diversified portfolio, Weleda is facing different challenges in terms of sub-supplier management and sustainability. One of the forthcoming challenges Weleda is facing is the general supply of quantity and quality. As most materials are vegetables, climatic influences and seasonal weather phenomena are a risk for Weleda's supply security. Weather conditions as well as human impact, like the use of pesticides, are having a significant influence on quantity and quality of the needed raw materials. Extreme summer and winter seasons in some cases are causing a complete shortage of yields.

On the other hand, the distribution, deposition, and drift of pesticides have more and more influence on product quality—even organic fields are contaminated. On top of the changing weather conditions come the working conditions in various countries that should be improved. Weleda's target is to set up fair business relationships with farmers, manufacturers, and distributors, according to the guidelines of the Union for Ethical BioTrade (UEBT).[1] Both changing weather conditions as a consequence of climate change and working conditions challenge Weleda's objective to ensure sustainably sourced raw materials. To guarantee this important customer proposition, Weleda needs full traceability of the whole supply chain to be able to implement actions for improvement.

## 3.3 Weleda's Sustainability Objectives Are Closely Related to Sub-supplier Performance

To overcome the challenges affecting Weleda's sourcing as well as its sustainability approach, it has set up a strategy:

> We are working for a world in which the health and beauty of people and nature continue to unfold. Weleda's high quality is the result of a sustainable business. Our targets: to create sustainable benefits for people and nature, to protect the diversity of nature and to inspire a sustainable lifestyle. (Weleda AG 2016)

In Table 1 are some vital elements of the strategy affecting Weleda's sourcing strategy and therefore as well its sub-supplier management.

[1] https://www.ethicalbiotrade.org/

**Table 1** Vital elements of the strategy affecting Weleda's sourcing strategy (Lotz et al. 2019)

| Active environmental protection | Responsible supply chain management |
|---|---|
| • Verified environmental management in accordance with EMAS and ISO 14001<br>• Steady expansion of renewable energies<br>• Reduction of greenhouse gas emissions<br>• Continuous energy efficiency measures<br>• Rigorous waste separation and recycling<br>• Steady improvement in water management<br>• Promotion of environmentally friendly mobility | • Long-standing cultivation partnerships and active support of local growers<br>• Systematic supply chain management in all supply chains for natural raw materials using the standards promulgated by the Union for Ethical BioTrade (UEBT) |
| Natural raw materials | Development and production |
| • Organically certified: over 80% of the plant-based raw materials<br>• Plant-based raw materials from biodynamic and organic cultivation as well as certified wild collection<br>• Eight Weleda medicinal plant gardens: around 30 ha with more than 300 types of plants<br>• Raw materials from more than 80 countries | • Fresh and direct processing of plants and raw materials<br>• Our own processing methods, inspired by anthroposophy<br>• Composition of our formulations based on the lead-plant concept<br>• Development of fragrances from natural essential oils<br>• Production of nearly all Weleda natural and organic cosmetics in Germany and Switzerland<br>• Production of Weleda pharmaceuticals mostly on-site |
| Control and quality | |
| • Highest possible transparency on the journey from the field to the product<br>• Regular personal auditing of suppliers<br>• Strict controls in our own analysis for all incoming raw materials and finished products<br>• GMP international pharmaceutical standards for pharmaceuticals and GMP rules for organic and natural cosmetics. Orientation towards high food standards in the residue control of natural and organic cosmetics | |

Source: Authors' own table

## 3.4 *Already Implemented Processes to Handle Challenges and Achieve Objectives*

To be able to meet the targets, Weleda has already implemented several management processes in the past. Every raw material and supply chain undergoes the process of international supplier release. This process is covering a big part in terms of traceability towards the second-tier supplier. With several questionnaires, direct suppliers as well as sub-suppliers have to prove their quality standards and fair working conditions. To be able to achieve full traceability from field to product and to get the reliable quantities and quality, Weleda started to implement the development of sub-suppliers—more exactly growers—several years ago. Nonetheless each of the development projects is slightly different due to the raw materials themselves, the farmers and growers, the situation in the farmer's country, or other exogenous reasons.

Sources of information for the risk assessment of every supply chain are information gained from documentation and questionnaires as well as experience from developing sub-suppliers and, of course, the know-how of every strategic purchaser. This risk assessment is carried out annually with the outcome of specific measurements to implement preventive, risk-reducing actions.

### 3.5 Potential and Requirements Regarding Improvement and Development of Practices and Processes

Although Weleda has processes like the abovementioned already implemented, it is facing difficulties in the reliable supply of quantities and quality. Both quantity and quality are critical success factors and needed to perform further actions and improvements at the supplier base. Moreover, although gained information of both processes is part of Weleda's risk assessment, the past showed that an understanding of the whole supply chain and its several actors would have been helpful to act proactively in situations of shortage and implement preventive actions instead of firefighting due to the escalation of the supply shortage.

To be able to act proactively, it is crucial to identify black boxes along the supply chain to solve the problem at its basis. The already implemented risk assessment process is helpful, but still it is not detailed enough as managers can't consider sub-suppliers on a lower supply chain tier. Besides identifying black boxes and bottlenecks to overcome shortages and quality issues, it is essential to be aware of them to improve working conditions of sub-suppliers.

## 4 Customizing the Future Sub-supplier Management Process Framework at Weleda

Therefore, it is necessary to extend the risk assessment process up to a sub-supplier level. But not only integration of the sub-suppliers into risk assessment is needed, also personal capabilities, e.g., intercultural, intellectual, and social skills of each strategic buyer, are playing an important role to gain the required information and implement action plans for improvement.

The intensive analysis of Weleda's supply chains has shown that sub-supplier management will play an essential role in upcoming challenges concerning sourcing and sustainability. Sub-supplier management is seen as a critical success factor to guarantee the source of quantity and quality corresponding to Weleda's sustainability targets in the future (Fig. 4).

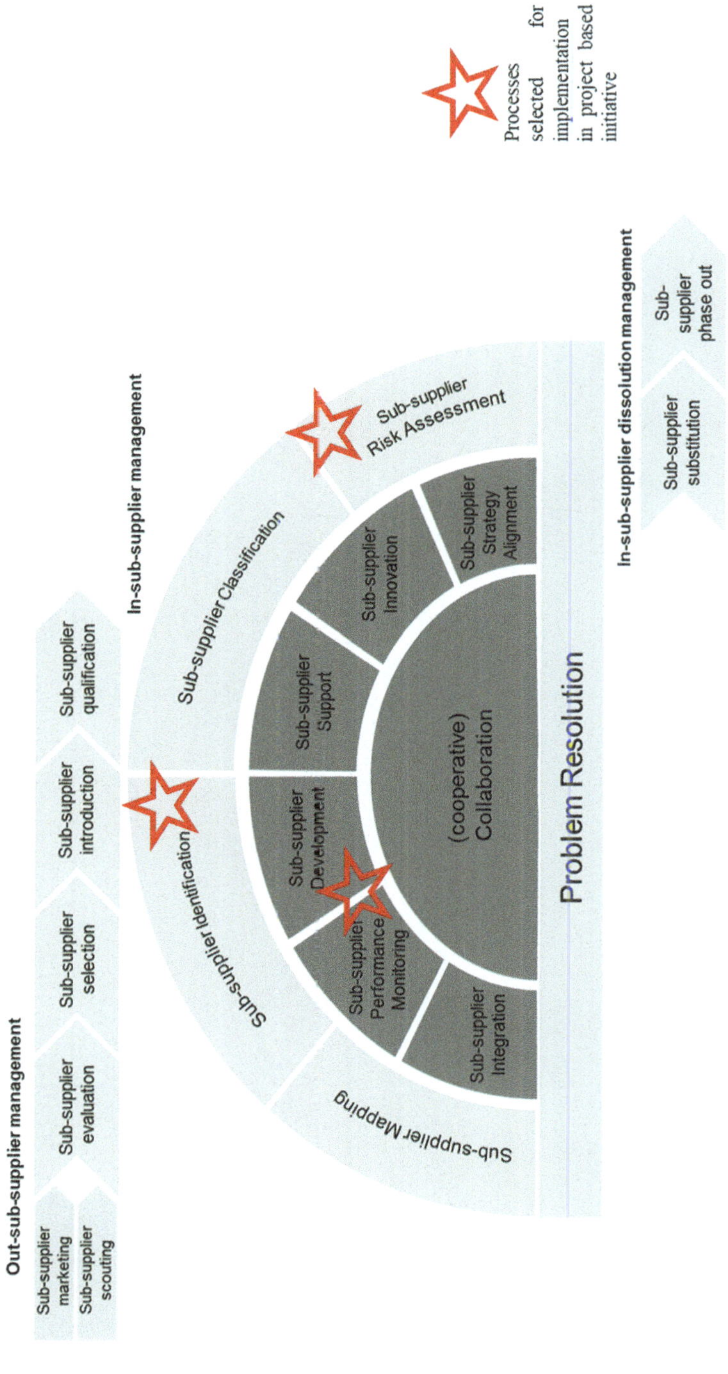


**Fig. 4** Sub-supplier management process framework (2). Source: Authors' own illustration

## Reference

Hofstetter JS (2018) Extending management upstream in supply chains beyond direct suppliers. IEEE Eng Manag Rev 46:106–116

# Sub-supplier Management Capabilities

**Julia Burkhardt**

**Abstract** For the last years, buyers concentrated on managing their direct suppliers, ignoring the much bigger share of suppliers beyond the direct supplier level. However, through a paradigm change in the market, the topic of the performance of sub-suppliers has become more important. In order for sub-supplier management to work effectively, firms require special internal and external capabilities. This chapter identifies the core capabilities needed for a successful management of sub-suppliers and includes some examples from the industry. It also derives recommendations for successfully implementing sub-supplier management capabilities from these examples.

The expanding outsourcing activities and a shift of value creation along the supply chain led to higher complexity and a lack of transparency in the supply chain. Buying companies are starting to lose the control over their own supply chain. Over the last years, buyers concentrated on managing their direct suppliers, ignoring the much bigger share of suppliers beyond the direct supplier level. However, through a paradigm change in the market, the topic of the performance in the supply chain beyond the direct supplier increased. This led to a change in the market, and many companies tried to start the implementation of sub-supplier management in their organization. However, the unstructured attempt to implement functioning sub-supplier management from scratch is bound to fail. The CTI project at hand, which has been executed with several firms from Switzerland, clearly detected that firms that want to implement sub-supplier management first require special capabilities to be able to make valuable use of implementing sub-supplier management.

J. Burkhardt (✉)
Institute of Supply Chain Management, University of St. Gallen, St. Gallen, Switzerland
e-mail: julia.burkhardt@unisg.ch

© The Author(s), under exclusive license to Springer Nature Switzerland AG 2021

W. Stoelzle, J. Burkhardt (eds.), *Sub-Supplier Management*, Contributions to Management Science, https://doi.org/10.1007/978-3-030-75575-1_4

# 1 Core Capabilities for the Successful Management of Sub-suppliers

Organizations that would like to dive into sub-supplier management require additional capabilities than the ones they already built up for managing their direct suppliers. Organizations seek capabilities to enable them to enhance their firm performance (Hayes and Pisano 1994; Lado et al. 1992). Capabilities are defined as the ability of a corporation to perform a coordinated set of tasks or the ability of utilizing organizational resources for the purpose of achieving a particular end result. "Distinctive capabilities are based on superiority in process management, integration of knowledge, and diffusion of learning" (Tracey et al. 2005). Especially capabilities in supply chain activities have become more important as they are seen as factors to strengthen competitiveness and to create sustainable competitive advantage as they can lead to superior customer value (Cooper et al. 1997; Tracey et al. 2005). Capabilities in supply chain management positively affect key competitive dimensions (Tracey et al. 2005). Hence, it is also of importance that companies generate sub-supplier-specific capabilities. The complexity of sub-supplier management begins with the fact that buyers are often not aware of who their sub-suppliers are, as transparency in the supply chain is hardly ever given. In the context of sub-supplier management, 4 categories were identified in over 20 workshops with 4 partners from various industries over the course of 2 years. The identified categories are (1) organizational structure and competences, (2) soft skills, (3) IT systems and processes, and (4) industry competence. The experience with the four companies led to the conclusion that the four categories influence each other and are interconnected. Each of the capabilities positively affects the other category, and the better a firm operates in one section, the more they strengthen the performance of the company (see Fig. 1).

## *1.1 Organizational Structure and Competences*

1. Top Management Support and Commitment
   One of the most critical points in sub-supplier management is the support of the top management for the topic. This requires a management that is oriented towards long-term thinking. One important success factor in this context is the provision of new staff positions or job enrichment. As the topic of sub-supplier management is not yet standardized, the top management should have tolerance for errors in the beginning of the implementation of practices. Top management support includes commitment of the management to the topic. If there is a lack of top management support, the topic can be addressed by a bottom-up process. Presenting business cases to the management is an effective method to obtain their support.

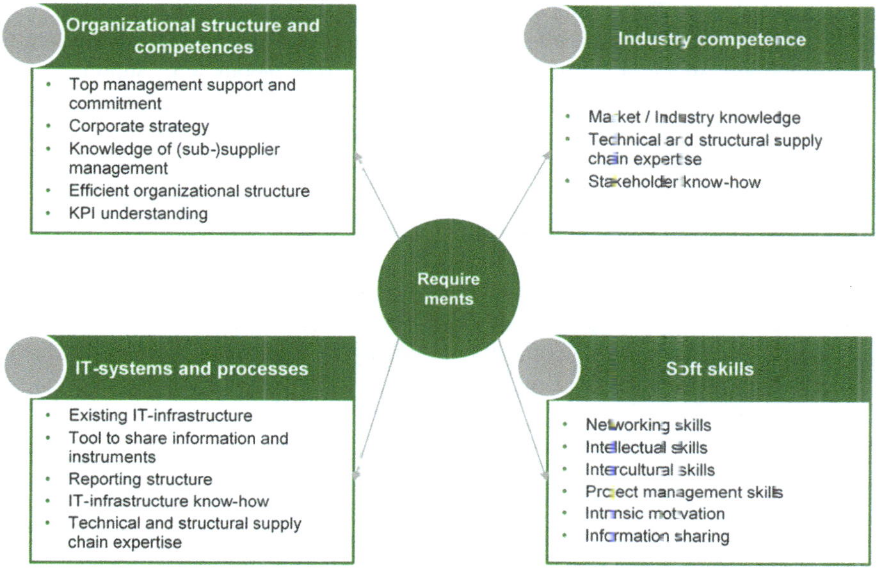


**Fig. 1** Core competencies for the successful management of sub-suppliers. Source: Authors' own illustration

2. Corporate Strategy

   Alongside with the top management support, companies should formulate a corporate strategy that includes the management of sub-suppliers to guarantee a consistent coordinated company strategy. Communicating this strategy is quite important in order to ensure that all employees are familiar with group targets and goals.

3. Procurement Market Strategy

   Besides adding sub-supplier management to the corporate strategy, the management also establishes a procurement market strategy. All employees should get access to this procurement market strategy to get familiar with goals and long-term orientation. Communication is also quite important to obtain this capability.

4. Information Management

   One critical capability is the one of company-wide information sharing in interdisciplinary departments that is accessible for every one that is interested in them. This also includes giving employees access to the corporate strategy to make sure they are familiar with group targets and goals.

5. KPI Understanding

   Management has defined KPIs in the context of sub-supplier management. They are shared with the employees, and it is made sure that employees understand which KPIs influence overall goals of relevant sub-supplier management. To obtain this, capability training and clear communication are beneficial.

6. Knowledge of (Sub-) Supplier Management

   Apart from knowing who the different suppliers are, it is also important to categorize them. In order to gain knowledge about the suppliers and sub-suppliers, the techniques of supplier mapping or supplier identification can be used. Furthermore, standardized schemes for the categorization of suppliers are implemented.
7. Knowledge of Resources

   The knowledge of resources comprises the clear communication on existing resources. The employees know which resources are required for sub-supplier management. To obtain this, capability project planning and management experience are two possible methods. Market research and reference visits can also contribute to the obtainment of this capability if there is a lack of knowledge of resources inside the company.
8. Commitment

   The commitment of management and staff to the topic is essential when trying to establish successful sub-supplier management. This includes a conflict culture, in which existing conflicts are solved constructive. Moreover, information transparency and company-wide communication of goals and targets are crucial. The definition of scope on the topic of sub-supplier management and of standard processes is helpful to obtain this capability. Success potentials should also be recognized and perceived.
9. Authority to Decide

   The capability "authority to decide" includes openly accessible job descriptions and clearly assigned internal staff positions. Through an explicit job description and the assignment of responsibilities with a RACI matrix, this can be obtained. Process mapping also helps to determine responsibilities.
10. Efficient Organizational Structure

    For a successful implementation of the corporate strategy, organizational structures have to be established. This includes a corporate strategy and standard processes, which are defined company-wide and are accessible. In addition, the organizational structure defines competences and responsibilities. Another key point of an efficient organizational structure is the support of organizational learning.
11. Customer Orientation

    The benefit of customer orientation is to know where to put the focus considering the topic of sub-supplier management. This is extremely important, considering the limited resources a company faces. To expand the knowledge, stakeholders should be analyzed. In addition, the assignment of responsibilities exists.

## 1.2 Industry Competence

1. Stakeholder Know-How
   To compete in a global environment, it is important for employees to be aware of the stakeholders that need handling. Employees need to know who their stakeholders are. Additionally, they need special knowledge of their suppliers, and they need to know of their needs and features. This also includes target group knowledge. The analysis of the target group is essential as needs of the target group can be derived. This includes customers as well as suppliers.
2. Technical and Structural Supply Chain Expertise
   Employees possess the technical expertise to manage the sub-suppliers (e.g., understanding of existing IT tools). Employees should also be familiar of distinct features of used materials and products. In addition, it is important that employees are familiar with existing supply chains and according pitfalls in the supply chain. When they work in the procurement department, it is essential that they have special expertise in their field of work to be able to manage sub-suppliers. Otherwise, it will be difficult to understand the specific context in which the sub-supplier operates or to detect bottlenecks in the supply chain.
3. (Procurement) Market Knowledge
   Employees understand the industry and market context they are operating in. Employees are experienced in the procurement market. This includes that they understand the specific context they interact in (country particularities). Furthermore, they need to have knowledge of the product assortment they are responsible for. This means that they have to be familiar with supply chains and distinctive features and material. An incentive structure that enables employees to use, share, and expand their knowledge and experiences should be established. The development of knowledge could also be supported through benchmarking and fair visits.
4. Market/Industry Knowledge
   Understanding of the market and industry context the company operates in is essential for sub-supplier marketing, selection, and scouting. Other market actors and competitors should be familiar. The sourcing department gathers and provides information to employees. Also, employees with personal experience are perfect for the work in sub-supplier management.
5. Knowledge of Supplier Management
   The employees possess knowledge to classify their suppliers. They are able to establish transparency over the supply chain, detecting connections. Resulting from that, they gain experience to adequately manage the suppliers. To classify the suppliers, they have supporting tools like "knockout" criteria lists.
6. Special Expertise
   Employees have special expertise in their field of work (e.g., procurement), and they can make use of their skills regarding sub-supplier management. To obtain this capability, learning on the job and career models that encourage employees becoming an expert should be established.

## 1.3 IT Systems and Processes

1. Existing IT Infrastructure
   This includes usable tools and instruments to be able to perform sub-supplier management. The tools should be able to share information on sub-suppliers and sub-supplier specifics in the supply chain. Also, it should be possible to derive a reporting structure from the IT.
2. Reporting Structure
   Employees have access to reports and the reporting structure. In addition, there are communication channels employees can use for reporting purposes. Through top management support and the improvement of the existing reporting structure, a suitable one can be provided.
3. IT Infrastructure Know-How
   Employees have the know-how to establish and use the IT infrastructure which is required for sub-supplier management. The implementation of highly complicated tools should be accomplished by training and the support of self-learning. External service providers and consultancies can also help to obtain this capability.

## 1.4 Soft Skills

1. Social Competence
   In sub-supplier management, especially soft skills are important to work successfully in the supply chain. Social competence is one of the key aspects here. This includes the exchange of information and the ability to communicate the corporate strategy. In addition, the employees need to be capable to create good relationships with suppliers.
2. Intrinsic Motivation/Attitude
   Successful sub-supplier management requires an intrinsic motivation and attitude towards the topic. Entrepreneurial thinking helps to understand the need for sub-supplier management and the goals. This leads to a higher intrinsic motivation. Especially during the change process, intrinsic motivation and persistence are of great importance.
3. Intercultural Skills
   Communicating information, networking, and intercultural skills are capabilities that are essential when trying to be successful in the triad. Due to the diverse background of suppliers and sub-suppliers, intercultural sensitivity and the ability to speak several languages should be supported.
4. Intellectual Skills
   Intellectual skills like analytical skills, abstract thinking, being proactive, rational thinking, being able to concentrate, as well as flexibility and creativity

are essential to be successful at the workplace. Especially, the consciousness of the relevance of a risk is needed in sub-supplier management. Defining a set of risks, which is checked regularly, helps to obtain this capability.

5. Project Management Skills

   Experience in project management is also promising to be successful in sub-supplier management. Achieving goals under constraints such as time and budget is relevant. Communication skills, leadership skills, and problem-solving skills are also important abilities to handle complex sub-supplier management projects.

6. Information Sharing

   One key point of successful sub-supplier management is information transparency between departments. For example, it is mandatory to communicate the corporate strategy to all employees. Even though information sharing is very important, this only applies to relevant information in order to avoid information overload.

7. Methodical Expertise

   Through training and self-learning, all employees should become experts in their field of work and in using tools and methods that are required to manage sub-suppliers.

8. Negotiation Skills

   Employees need to have expertise in negotiations with suppliers or sub-suppliers, e.g., about contract terms. Managing contrary views and finding a solution that satisfies all parties are the basis for a successful relationship. For this, it is necessary to be able to listen carefully and to know how to influence people.

9. Organizational/Coordination Capabilities

   Every employee needs to share own knowledge and in return be willing to learn and expand the own knowledge. In addition, errors should be tolerated and used for further learning. For this, an incentive structure should be established, which enables the development of knowledge.

## 2 Recommendations: The Road to Sub-supplier Management Capabilities

Sub-supplier management requires numerous management capabilities. Companies first need to obtain these capabilities before sub-supplier management can be implemented successfully. These changes involve the development of employees, adjustments in organizational structure, provision of technical solutions, and extensive communication.

The aim of the development of employees is to provide new knowledge and competences the employees need for their new tasks. Training is an efficient method to obtain this aim. Specialist knowledge, technical expertise (e.g., about the IT tools), and soft skills should be part of this training. Another important requirement for a successful training is that all affected employees receive the required training and not only individuals. In addition, the training should be adapted to the individual level of knowledge. In the beginning of the implementation of practices, everyone should have tolerance for errors. Knowledge and competences can also be obtained through the support of self-learning and internal knowledge sharing.

If there are not enough personal resources for the implementation of sub-supplier management available in the company, new employees should be hired. These employees should be the “right” ones for the job concerning existing expertise, experiences, and knowledge.

Furthermore, successful sub-supplier management requires cooperation in cross-functional teams. Due to this cooperation, diverse expertise, knowledge, and competences are combined and can lead to better outcomes. To operate successfully, it is necessary to define clear objectives and to assign competences so they can decide independently concerning their tasks. In addition, each team member should identify with the team, which can be supported by team-building measures.

The implementation of sub-supplier management also comes along with adjustments in the organizational structure. First, the scope on the topic of sub-supplier management needs to be defined. Another important aspect is the definition and introduction of standardized processes and standardized process mapping. In addition, the allocation of tasks and responsibilities is also of great importance. Therefore, the roles should be defined without conflicts, and job descriptions are explicit and open to access. Tasks and responsibilities are allocated based on expertise, knowledge, and experience. An incentive structure, which enables information sharing, willingness to learn, and the development of required competences, is added.

Another important aspect for the implementation of successful sub-supplier management is the provision of necessary IT infrastructure. IT tools and instruments for reporting purposes and for the exchange of information need to be implemented. Due to the high complexity, the implementation of new IT tools should be accompanied by training and the support of self-learning.

The crucial aspect to obtain capabilities is communication. After the definition of a corporate strategy including sub-supplier management, this new strategy needs to be communicated to all employees to get familiar with group targets and goals. Moreover, the different departments should share information. It is important to limit information sharing to relevant pieces of information in order to prevent information overload.

## References[1]

Cooper M, Lambert D, Pagh JD (1997) Supply chain management: more than a new name for logistics. Int J Logist Manag 8(1):1–14

Hayes J, Pisano G (1994) Beyond world-class: the new manufacturing strategy. Harv Bus Rev 72:77–86

Lado A, Boyd N, Wright P (1992) A competency-based model of sustainable competitive advantage: toward a conceptual integration. J Manag 18:77–91

Tracey M, Lim J, Vonderembse M (2005) The impact of supply-chain management capabilities on business performance. Supply Chain Manag 10(3):179–191

[1]Furthermore: workshops and interviews within the Innosuisse project over the course of 2 years.

## References

# The Concept of Sub-supplier Specific Investments as a Development Tool

**Julia Burkhardt**

**Abstract** This chapter gives an overview of the concept of placing sub-supplier specific investments. Motivations of sub-supplier specific investments are discussed, and a classification of sub-suppliers is introduced. Interactions between the firm and the triad as well as the safeguarding of the firm's investment are evaluated, and an overview of internal and external barriers to the execution of sub-supplier specific investments is given.

Placing sub-supplier specific investments is a management tool in the process of sub-supplier development, as proposed in the framework of Hofstetter (2016) and depicted in Fig. 1.

As Burkhardt (2019) extracted:

> Sub-supplier specific investments are strategic, non-recoverable investments that a buyer places—incident driven or proactive—directly in his sub-supplier with the aim to develop a specific sub-supplier to increase supply chain performance.[1]

The following chapter will give an overview of the concept of placing sub-supplier specific investments, which is pictured in Fig. 2. The process of placing sub-supplier specific investments starts with the decision of companies to develop their sub-suppliers through placing sub-supplier specific investments. This can be driven through an incident in the supply chain or be proactively anticipated by companies. In contrast to incident-driven specific investments into the

The whole chapter is a modified extract from Julia Burkhardt (2019) Sub-supplier management—developing lower-tier supplier through sub-supplier specific investments, Dissertation no. 4879, Difo-Druck, Untersiemau.

[1]One common citation of performance measurement was developed by Neely, Gregory, and Platts (1995): "Performance measurement can be defined as the process of quantifying the efficiency and effectiveness of action." A positive performance is also achieved if the highest possible output is generated through the lowest input of resources (Burkhardt 2018).

J. Burkhardt (✉)
Institute of Supply Chain Management, University of St. Gallen, St. Gallen, Switzerland

© The Author(s), under exclusive license to Springer Nature Switzerland AG 2021 
W. Stoelzle, J. Burkhardt (eds.), *Sub-Supplier Management*, Contributions to Management Science, https://doi.org/10.1007/978-3-030-75575-1_5

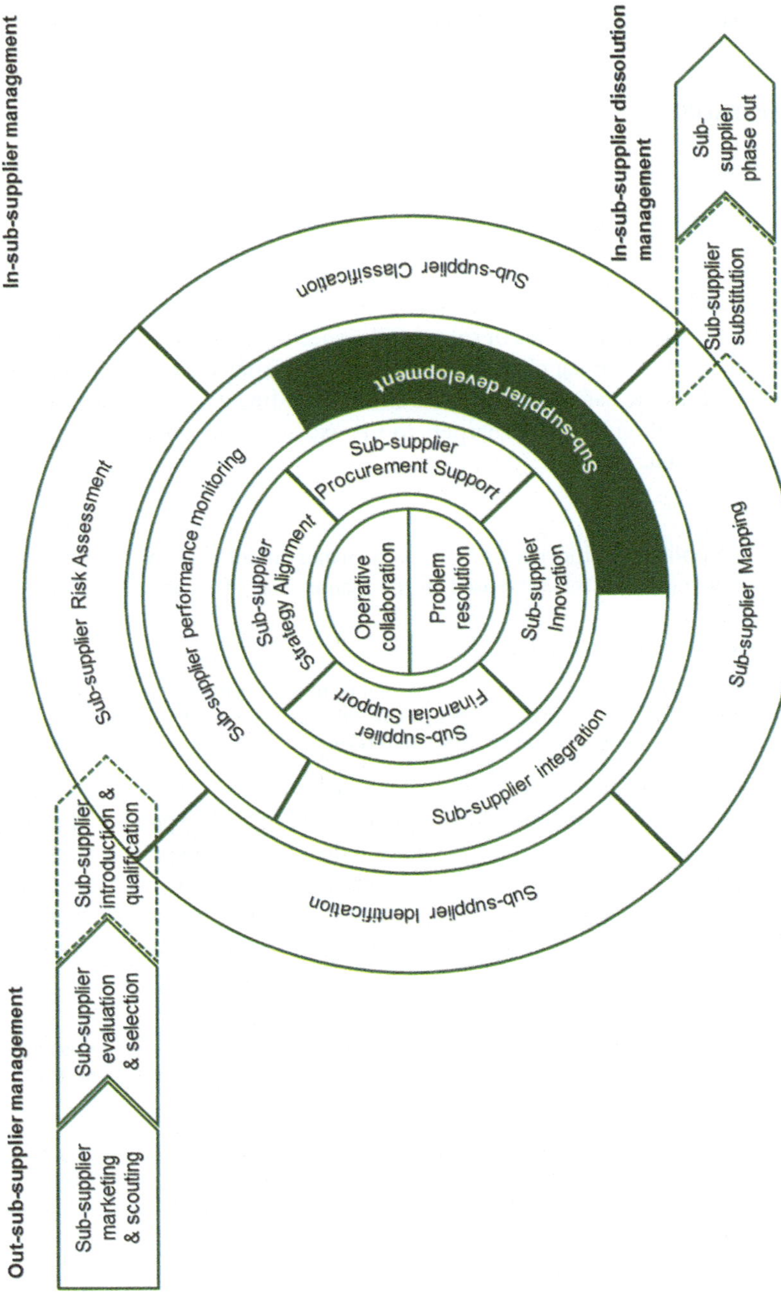


**Fig. 1** Framework of sub-supplier management (Hofstetter 2016)

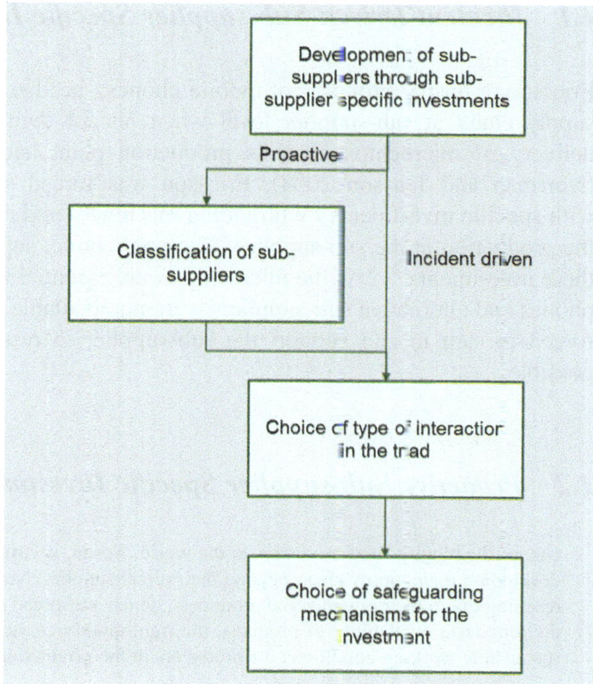


**Fig. 2** Process of placing sub-supplier specific investments (Burkhardt 2019)

sub-supplier, proactive sub-supplier specific investments require the classification and identification of the existing sub-supplier base. This will be further executed in Sect. 1. After the companies are aware of which sub-suppliers are in their supply chain, it is essential for them to choose a type of interaction with the supplier and their sub-supplier. Various options are further evaluated in Sect. 2. After the type of interaction for the triad is defined, it is important that the specific investments in the sub-supplier are safeguarded. An overview of safeguards and their usability is explained in Sect. 3. As sub-supplier specific investments come with various challenges, Sect. 4. sheds light on possible internal and external barriers that could prevent the execution of sub-supplier specific investments.

## 1 The Concept of Placing Sub-supplier Specific Investments as a Buyer

Experiences from practice emphasize two motivations of buying companies to place sub-supplier specific investments:

1. Incident-driven sub-supplier specific investments
2. Proactive sub-supplier specific investments

## 1.1 Incident-Driven Sub-supplier Specific Investments

Ericsson, a former producer of mobile phones, faced severe disruptions along their supply chain at sub-supplier level when one of their sub-suppliers stopped the delivery of microchips after its production plant had been destroyed in a fire (Norrman and Jansson 2004). Ericsson was forced supporting the sub-supplier with specific investments by providing machinery and monetary subsidies to restart the production at the sub-supplier. Ericsson's direct supplier was not able to cover these investments.[2, 3] As the microchips were essential for the production of mobile phones and alternative sub-suppliers were not available in the market, Ericsson was forced to step in and support the sub-supplier to restart production as quick as possible.

## 1.2 Proactive Sub-supplier Specific Investments

One of the biggest food producers in the world, Nestlé, is strongly involved in pro-actively developing their supply chain beyond their direct supplier. Nestlé has put a strong focus on reaching out to their raw material producers, which are spread across the globe, to guarantee the long-term availability of products, the right quality of the products as well as fair and sustainable working conditions for producers in the production process.[4]

One of Nestlé's projects is the development of coffee plantations in Ivory Cost or in the Philippines with sub-supplier specific investments. Initially, Nestlé had to attain actor-specific transparency in their supply chain by identifying from which farmers they actually purchase their coffee beans. After the initial identification, Nestlé was able to directly contact the raw material producers (coffee bean farmers). In order to ensure availability and quality level and guarantee fair working conditions actively, Nestlé concentrated on the transferring of knowledge, provision of equipment, and training of farmers in growing and maintaining coffee beans. In doing so, Nestlé placed sub-supplier specific investments in the identified farmers. These direct investments in the coffee bean producers were possible only because the direct suppliers revealed the identity of their suppliers to Nestlé (Burkhardt 2019).

To sum it up again, a buying firm is either forced to place sub-supplier specific investments due to an incident in the supply chain, or it plans to proactively develop the sub-supplier or his supply chain through placing sub-supplier specific

[2]Extracted from Burkhardt (2019).

[3]The whole case can be read in Norrman and Jansson (2004).

[4]The paragraph about Nestlé used information retrieved from sources that have been provided by Nestlé on their website: Nestlé in society. Creating Shared Value and meeting our commitments 2016. Full report, 2017 (https://www.nestle.com/asset-library/documents/library/documents/corporate_social_responsibility/nestle-in-society-summary-report-2016-en.pdf).

investments. As demonstrated by the Ericsson case, developing sub-suppliers through an incident in the supply chain is often the "last resort" to keep the supply chain from disrupting. The situation is different when buying companies decide to place sub-supplier specific investments proactive. Buying firms apply sub-supplier specific investments as a development tool for their supply chain. In contrast to incident-driven investments into the supply chain, the buyer faces more options when deciding to place sub-supplier specific investments. The initial question for buying companies is which sub-suppliers they should develop.

## 2 Classification of Sub-suppliers for Proactive Sub-supplier Specific Investments

The "classification of the sub-supplier" helps to classify the existing sub-supplier base. It is crucial for the success of placing sub-supplier specific investments as buyers. This process is also described in the sub-supplier management framework of Hofstetter (see his working paper "Towards a Process Framework for Sub-supplier Management," 2016). The developed classification process follows the known Kraljic matrix (1983) with the two assorted specifications "criticality of the sub-supplier" and "probability of success" (Fig. 3).

### *2.1 The Criticality of the Sub-supplier*

The performance in the supply chain is dependent on each member of the supply chain (Choi and Kim 2008). This is true for the supplier and can also be extended to the sub-supplier level; hence, when a sub-supplier performs poorly, this influences the performance of the first-tier supplier as well. Research pointed to four decisive points that define the criticality of sub-suppliers.

1. The criticality of a sub-supplier increases if he is of strategic importance for the supply chain, hence for the buyer or the suppliers. As Hult et al. (2004) state, a supply chain is critical, when "members are strategically, operationally, and technologically integrated." If the sub-supplier has a substantial impact on a buying firm's profit, they are rated as critical. One example for that would be that the sub-supplier provides a critical product component, or the sub-supplier has a technological advantage that is required at the supplier or buyer level (Borgatti and Li 2009). If the sub-supplier is using innovative and complex technology, he is likely to be a single source sub-supplier and hence becomes strategically important for supplier and buyer. Just as in the dyad, the more complicated it is to replace the sub-supplier, the more important he becomes for the success of the supply chain. Another point that increases the criticality of the sub-supplier is how much the sub-supplier increases risks in the supply chain for

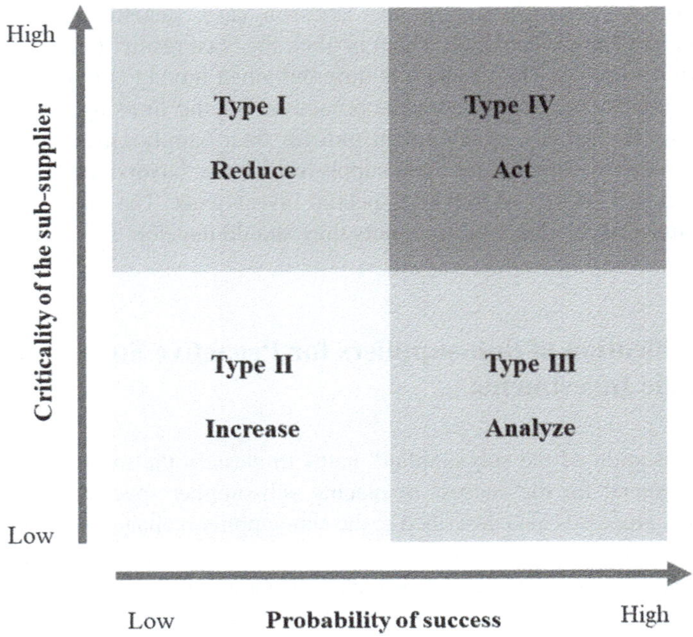


**Fig. 3** Classification of sub-suppliers for placing sub-supplier specific investments. Source: Authors' own illustration

the buying firm, e.g., due to their country base or development of their production site (Yan et al. 2015; Kraljic 1983).

2. The criticality of a sub-supplier also increases if the supplier is a nexus supplier. A nexus supplier is characterized by a consolidation of various supply chain nodes at one supplier. That means that one sub-supplier delivers their products to several suppliers in the supply chain. If this sub-supplier comes into financial trouble or is hit by an environmental catastrophe, this will influence the entire supply chain (Yan et al. 2015). If this is the case, the sub-supplier becomes very strategic and, hence, critical for the buyer. If this sub-supplier performs poorly, it would affect multiple suppliers in the supply chain, making it challenging for the buyer to switch suppliers to avoid the problem. Thus, a failure of a nexus sub-supplier could result in multiple performance gaps in the buyers supply chain (Yan et al. 2015) (Fig. 4).
3. The criticality of a sub-supplier is increased if it offers a unique and innovative technology that is required to improve the overall performance of the finished good (Yan et al. 2015).
4. The criticality of a sub-supplier is also increasing depending on where he is located in the supply chain. This can be positively related, e.g., if he is able to open specific markets or cultures for the supplier or the buyer (Hitt et al. 2000). However, sub-suppliers can also become critical due to the country they are

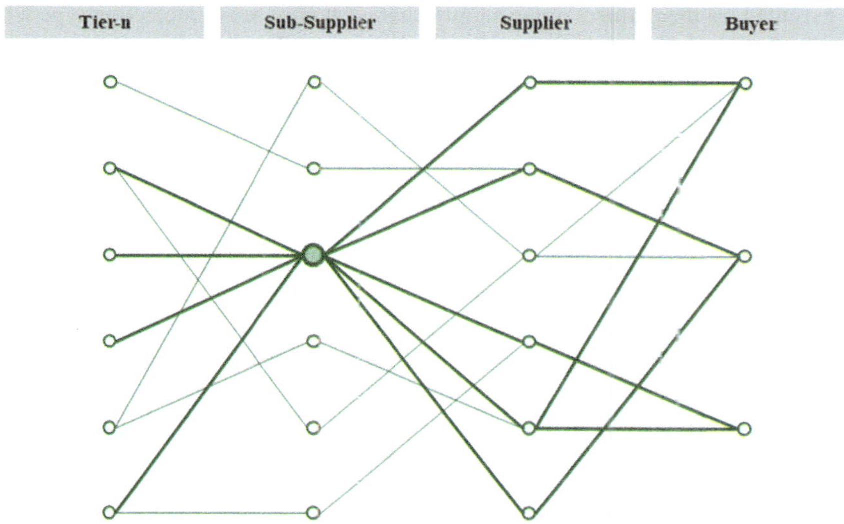


**Fig. 4** Position of the nexus supplier in the supply chain network. Source: Authors' own illustration

located in. Countries with political instability can suddenly change their trade agreements and thus endanger demanded supply. Climate changes in specific regions of the world make reliable continuation of the business critical. Some markets are highly protected, and having a good relationship with someone present in the market can allow the buyer to get an overview and access to the market.

## 2.2 *The Probability of Success when Placing Sub-supplier Specific Investments*

*The probability of success* describes the rate of probability that the specific investments placed in the sub-supplier lead to the results that the buyer intended. The empirical research at hand revealed that the probability of success is dependent on five contextual factors that are presented in the following paragraphs.

1. First, the relationship with the direct supplier is a key factor. The relationship of the buyer with his direct supplier influences the type of interactions that are possible in the triad. When the buyer wants to expand his management down the triad through sub-supplier specific investments, he must involve his direct supplier, and they need to reach consensus regarding which type of interaction will be useful. The more intense and trustful the relationship between the buyer and his supplier, the more likely that sub-supplier specific investments can be

executed, as the partners in the supply chain can choose an interaction type with open communication between the three parties. The supplier does not feel threatened by the buyer, and the buyer does not need to fear that the supplier will end the relationship with his direct supplier (the buyer's sub-supplier), which would turn executed investments into sunk costs. Here, the empirical investigation at hand also showed that cultural and regional closeness between buyer and sub-supplier positively influences the results of the sub-supplier specific investment.

2. If the buyer has identified a nexus supplier, he can assume that managing the nexus supplier is rather complicated. A dependence on the buying firm from the perspective of the nexus supplier is mostly nonexistent; however, the buying company is dependent on the nexus supplier, as the nexus supplier is strategic due to their nodes in the supply chain (Yan et al. 2015). Hence, they do not see a need to form long-term relationships with buyers. The probability of success in managing these sub-suppliers is therefore relatively low. Furthermore, in this constellation, buyers are always confronted with the fact that their sub-supplier specific investments will benefit other buying firms as well. Thus, buying firms would rather wait until other buyers start investing.
3. By contrast, the more dependent the sub-supplier is on the buyer, the more likely it is that placing sub-supplier specific investment will lead to the results the buyer intended. The more dependent a supplier or a sub-supplier is on the buyer, the more likely it is that sub-supplier specific investments will not be abused by one of the supply chain partners and hence will not be lost.
4. Probability of success is also dependent on whether or not it is a first-time investment by the buyer into a sub-supplier. The more frequently a buyer invests in lower-tier suppliers, the more likely it is that the outcome of the sub-supplier specific investments will be positive for him. If the situation of placing sub-supplier specific investments, including reaching out to sub-suppliers or involving suppliers in the considerations, becomes routine, it is more likely that sub-supplier specific investments will result in a positive outcome.
5. A last point that positively influences the probability of success of a specific investment is the strategic alignment between buyer, supplier, and sub-supplier. The more evolved the strategic consent in the triad regarding business orientation, the higher the probability of success for the placed investment.

After determining the probability of the success and the criticality of the sub-supplier, buyers can place their existing sub-suppliers' base in the matrix. The classification matrix, as presented in Fig. 5, is segmented into four quadrants:

- Type I: Reduce
- Type II: Increase
- Type III: Analyze
- Type IV: Act

In the following section, the four quadrants will be discussed in more depth.

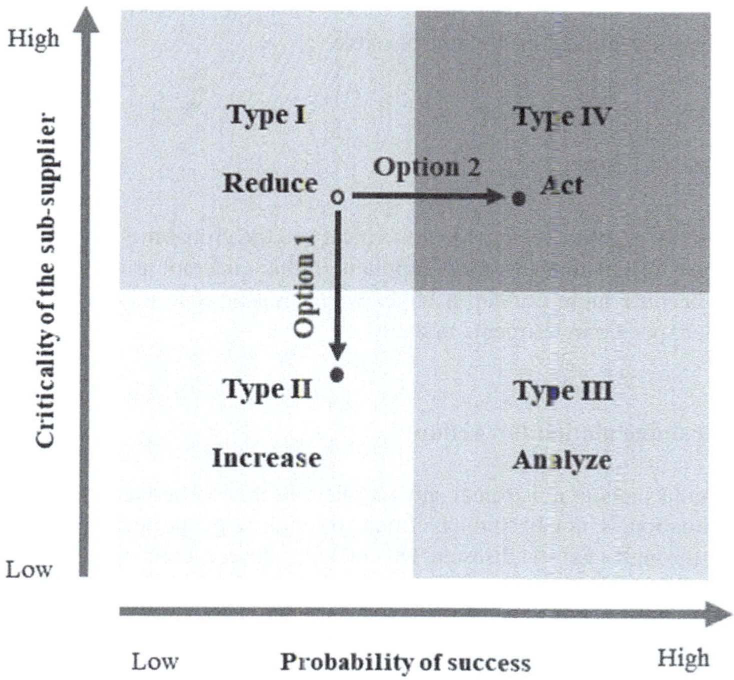


**Fig. 5** Type I recommendation for action. Source: Authors' own illustration

## 2.3 *Type I: Reduce*

Sub-suppliers in this quadrant must be carefully considered by the buyer when he considers to place sub-supplier specific investments. The buyer is confronted with a strategically or financially important sub-supplier, maybe even a nexus supplier. Therefore, it makes sense for the buyer to emphasize his commitment, but the probability of success is limited, as the buyer either does not have a strong relationship with his direct supplier, or the sub-supplier is blocking interactions (e.g., he is too powerful: nexus supplier).

### 2.3.1 Recommendation for Action

In this quadrant it should be the priority for the buyer to reduce the criticality of his sub-supplier. The buyer has two options in this quadrant. First of all, he could try to implement a second source to decrease the criticality of one sub-supplier. This would reduce the criticality of the sub-supplier and move him to quadrant II. If this is not feasible, the buyer should try to improve the relationship with the sub-supplier, be it through the direct supplier or directly. This would move the sub-supplier to quadrant

IV. Both scenarios are very cost intense for the buyer. It is recommended to have as few sub-suppliers in this quadrant as possible.

## 2.4 *Type II: Increase*

The sub-suppliers in this section are not critical and the probability of success is low. Possible risks originating from sub-suppliers in this quadrant are low; however, in case they become more critical, a buyer would not be able to successfully place sub-supplier specific investments in them.

### 2.4.1 Recommendation for Action

Buyers should include noncritical sub-suppliers in their observations to make sure that the situation is not becoming critical through, e.g., political instability in a country or through a natural disaster. This includes observations of the whole supply chain and observation of market developments, which could influence the role of the sub-supplier. Furthermore, buyers should consider to increase the probability of success in the long term to be prepared if the sub-suppliers should ever become critical for their supply chain (slowly move them towards quadrant III) (Fig. 6).

## 2.5 *Type III: Analyze*

The probability of success for placing sub-supplier specific investments is very high in this quadrant, but the sub-suppliers in this quadrant are not critical for the buyer. Hence, there is no need for the buyer to activate sub-supplier specific investments in a sub-supplier that is not important for the buyer, be it strategically or economically.

### 2.5.1 Recommendation for Action

In this quadrant, it is necessary that the buyer analyzes how much resources (time and money) he currently spends on maintaining the relationship between himself and the supplier and the sub-supplier. If this evaluation shows that the good relationship only originates through disproportionate resources from the buyer, he should try to reduce the amount of effort invested in the supplier or the sub-supplier without significantly decreasing the probability of success. The sub-supplier should remain in quadrant III, so in case he ever turns critical, the buyer already has a high probability that his sub-supplier specific investments turn out the way the buyer intends (Fig. 7).

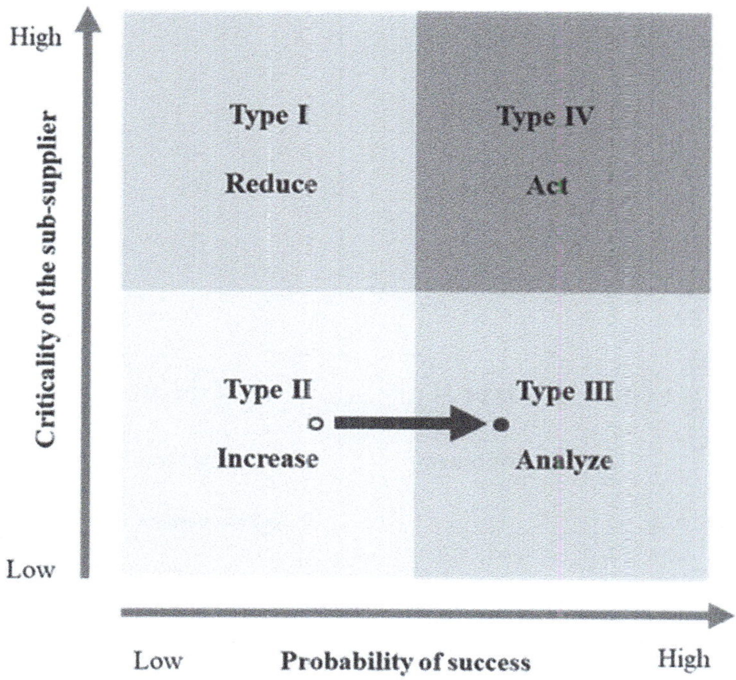


**Fig. 6** Type II recommendation for action. Source: Authors' own illustration

## 2.6 *Type IV: Act*

Sub-suppliers in this quadrant are highly critical for the buyer, and the probability of success for placing sub-supplier specific investments is high. The sub-supplier is financially, strategically, or economically important, and the probability that sub-supplier specific investments will lead to the expected outcome is high. Furthermore, if the buyer did not invest in the sub-supplier in this quadrant, it could also have a negative impact on his supply chain as the sub-suppliers in this quadrant have a high impact on the supply chain of the buyer.

### 2.6.1 Recommendation for Action

In this quadrant the buyer has two options. He could try to reduce the criticality of the sub-supplier, by trying to build up second sources long term. If this is not possible, the buyer should initiate contact with the sub-suppliers in this quadrant and decide with them how they could ensure that their criticality does not negatively affect the supply chain of the buyer in the future. One option to strenghten the supply chain is placing sub-supplier specific invesments in the identified critical sub-

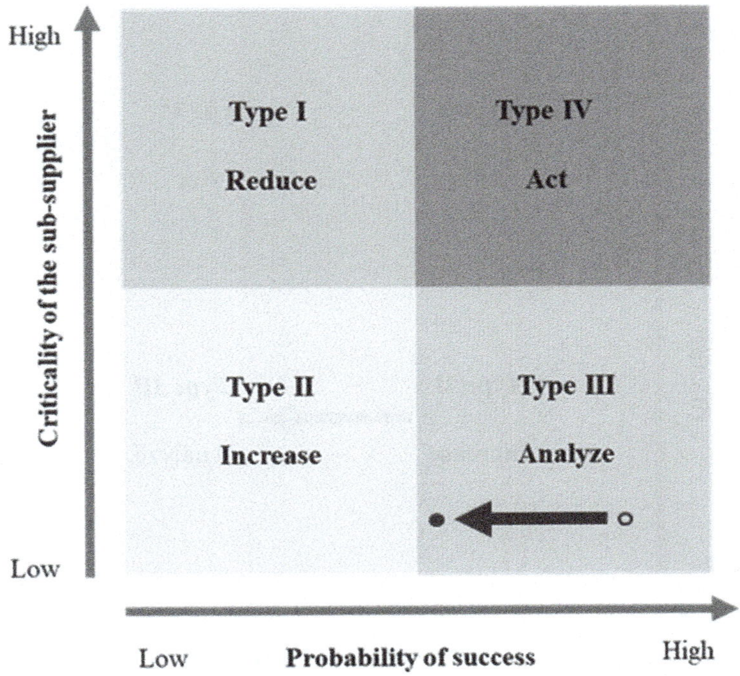


**Fig. 7** Type III recommendation for action. Source: Authors' own illustration

suppliers. This is mostly implemented with the support of the direct supplier and the sub-supplier, as options to place sub-supplier specific investments need to be evaluated by the supply chain partners together. In fact, quadrant IV is the only quadrant where it is recommended to make use of sub-supplier specific investments as a proactive sub-supplier management approach. As the relationship between buyer and supplier is strong, the buyer may gain access to innovation through sub-suppliers in this quadrant, and they might develop potential innovations together (Fig. 8).

## 3 Choice of Interaction Type in the Triad with According Safeguarding Mechanisms

A buyer can choose between eight different types of interaction when considering placing sub-supplier specific investments. Some of the interaction types are only existing in the context of incident-driven sub-supplier specific investments, e.g., "Single Soldier," "Ambush," or "Joint Purpose." The remaining five can be found in proactive and incident-driven context. These five interaction types were first developed by Hofstetter (2016). Regardless of interaction type, a buying firm should

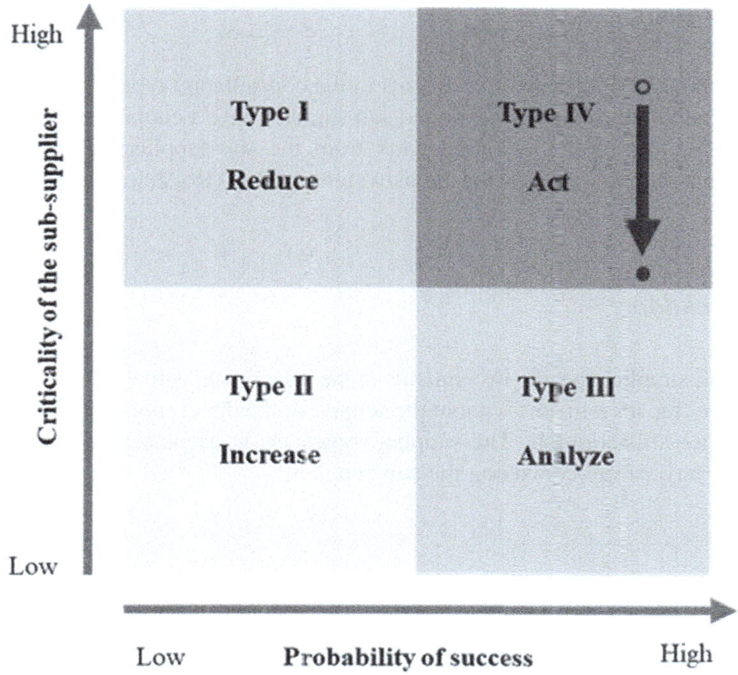


**Fig. 8** Type IV recommendation for action. Source: Authors' own illustration

always safeguard their sub-supplier specific investments (Williamson 1991). For the purpose of safeguarding specific investments, the buyer can choose between formal [e.g., contract or written agreement (Williamson 1991)] and informal safeguarding mechanisms [e.g., relationship age, trust between business partners (MacNeil 1980; Rob and Yang 2010)].

The relationship the buyer has with his supplier and sub-supplier determines the type of interaction that is chosen when placing sub-supplier specific investments. In the following paragraphs, the eight different interaction types are briefly described.

## 3.1 Cooperation

Placing sub-supplier specific investments in a cooperation describes the direct cooperation between buyer—supplier and sub-supplier. They are most likely sitting at the same table and making decisions together in the triad. In this scenario, the buyer, the supplier, and the sub-supplier have a long and trustful relationship (Hofstetter 2016).

## 3.2 *Parallel*

Placing sub-supplier specific investments in the constellation type "Parallel" means buyer and supplier, as well as buyer and sub-supplier have a cooperative interaction. The supplier only orders standard parts from the sub-supplier; hence, it is not required that they have a close or intensive relationship (Hofstetter 2016).

## 3.3 *Backdoor*

Placing sub-supplier specific investments in the "Backdoor" situation means that the buyer places the investments without the support of the direct supplier, as they do not have a close collaboration. The supplier, however, is irreplaceable and does not hinder the buyer from contacting the sub-supplier.

## 3.4 *Double Agency*

Placing sub-supplier specific investments in the "Double Agency" situation means that the buyer places the investments with an arm's length relationship with his sub-supplier. They do not have close contact. However, the buyer and the supplier, as well as the supplier and the sub-supplier, have close interactions.

## 3.5 *Bypass*

Placing sub-supplier specific investments in a "Bypass" situation can develop when the supplier is not replaceable in the supply chain. The supplier is not interested in becoming more involved in the supply chain and does not mind that the buyer has direct contact with the sub-supplier as he is assured that his position in the supply chain is safe. He is irreplaceable (Hofstetter 2016).

## 3.6 *Single Soldier*

Placing sub-supplier specific investments in the "Single Soldier" situation describes the cooperative relationship of the buyer with his direct supplier. The buyer and his direct supplier both only have an arm's length relationship with the sub-supplier. This type of constellation situation should be avoided.

## 3.7 Ambush

Placing sub-supplier specific investments in the "Ambush" situation means that the buyer has an arm's length relationship with his supplier as well as with his sub-supplier. The supplier has a cooperation with the sub-supplier. This could be due to historical connectedness and can be often found when the supplier and the sub-supplier have one parent company. The investment is only executed to avoid a production stop.

## 3.8 Joint Purpose

The constellation type "Joint Purpose" describes the scenario where all partners in the triad have an arm's length relationship with one another. This is the worst possible scenario for placing sub-supplier specific investments and should always be avoided if possible.

As Fig. 9 shows, some of the interaction types are only chosen when the companies are forced to act due to an incident-driven sub-supplier specific investment. In an incident-driven scenario, the sub-supplier specific investments are likely to be used to avoid a disruption of the supply chain. Hence, buyers place the sub-supplier specific investments to avoid even bigger costs in the long run. Be it incident-driven or proactively, it is nevertheless important that buying firms try to safeguard their sub-supplier specific investments as the buyer and the sub-supplier usually have no contractual agreements between each other. For this purpose, buyer can choose between formal and informal safeguarding mechanisms.

## 3.9 Formal Safeguards

The most prevalent formal safeguards include a contract or written agreement between two parties (Williamson 1985). Although contracts and written agreements can be incomplete, they are the most commonly used form of safeguards between two parties (Cannon et al. 2000). They are also applicable in the triadic setting, between buyer and sub-supplier, to safeguard specific investments.

## 3.10 Informal Safeguards

The best-known informal safeguards are trust, relationship age, or building financial hostages between two parties. Trust in business partners results from experiences the buyer has had with his sub-supplier in the past or the experiences his direct supplier

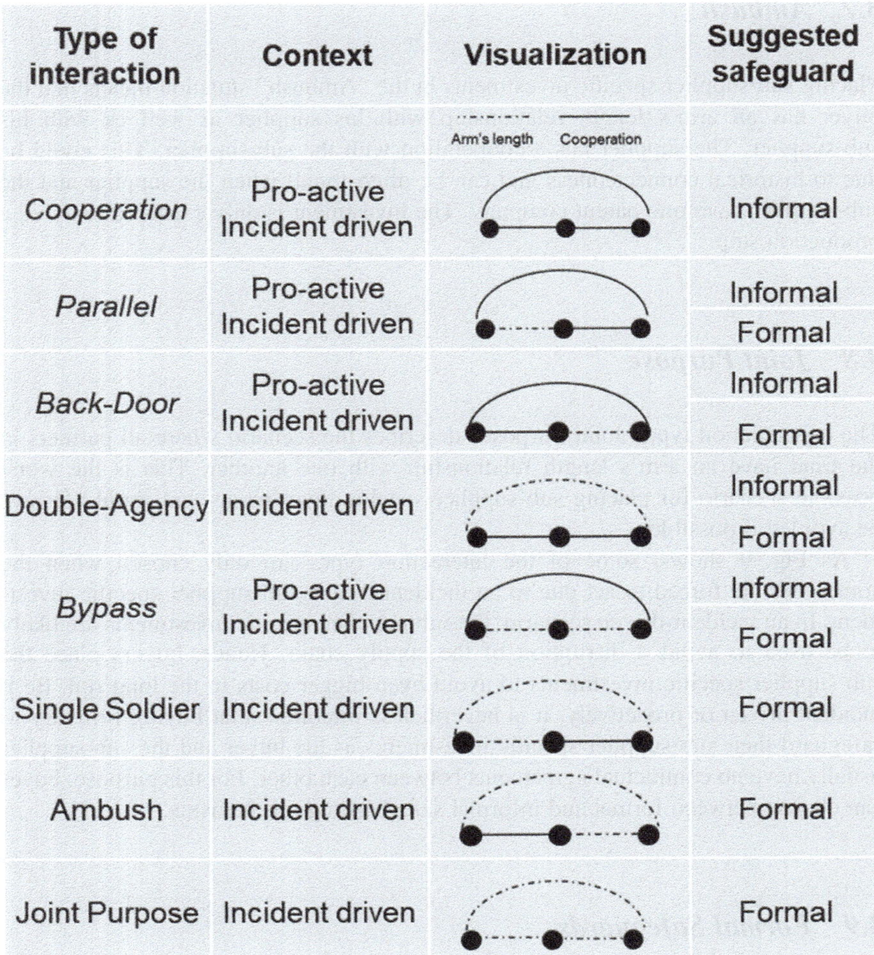


**Fig. 9** Interaction types for sub-supplier management. Source: Authors' own illustration

has had with sub-suppliers in the past that he shares with the buyer (Ebers and Semrau 2015). Having long-term relationships between buyer, supplier, and sub-supplier is associated with mutual trust and appreciation between business partners. Furthermore, long-term relationships are often found in dependent relationships. If the business partners are dependent on one another, they will try to maintain the relationship and will make sure that the specific investments are not lost (Wagner and Bode 2013).

# 4 Internal and External Barriers for Placing Sub-supplier Specific Investments as a Buyer

As mentioned before, sub-supplier specific investments are quite cost intense for buying firms. It is only natural that there are several resentments against placing them. Observations from practice showed that buyers are faced with external and internal barriers to place sub-supplier specific investments.

## 4.1 *Internal Barriers*

- *Lack of Top Management Support*: If the management of a buying company is resistant to managing the supply chain beyond the direct supplier, the process to change the attitude of the management will be quite challenging. Top management can have several reasons to be defensive towards sub-supplier specific investments. It requires a lot of resources, the outcome is mostly not quantifiable, and management does not see the buyer as being responsible for managing the sub-supplier as they have a supplier in the supply chain.
- *Resource Shortage of the Buyer*: Placing sub-supplier specific investments (incident-driven or proactive) requires available resources at the buyer's site that buyers are willing to spend to develop the sub-supplier.
- *Transparency on Sub-suppliers*: Be it an incident-driven or a proactive investment in sub-suppliers, the buyer must always be aware of who the sub-supplier is. Often, he does not have this information. To detect the sub-suppliers, buyers can make use of service providers, e.g., providers that help the buyers to map the supply chain. If the buyer or a service provider is not able to identify sub-suppliers in the supply chain, the buyer has no opportunity to invest in his sub-suppliers.
- *Resistance of the Employees:* A proactive involvement of buyers in the supply chain on the sub-supplier level is not obvious for employees. They are rather overburdened by the prospect of additional tasks and working hours without obvious results. Avoiding risks that have not taken place yet is counterintuitive for many employees. As a result, employees can react with resistance to additional tasks. An additional aspect could be that sub-suppliers are often located in an international context. This could cross the comfort line of many employees, as working in different cultural zones with different backgrounds can be intimidating for them. They may also react with resistance.

## 4.2 External Barriers

- *Supplier or Sub-supplier Block Working Together with the Buyer*: An extreme barrier could be, for example, if a supplier tries to prevent any attempt by the buyer to contact their sub-supplier. This situation arises when the supplier is afraid that an interaction between buyer and sub-supplier will lead to a loss of his relevance in the supply chain and that he could be replaced with the sub-supplier. Another reason for the supplier to block the connection between buyer and sub-supplier could be that they are trying to prevent the cost composition of their product from becoming questionable. Sub-suppliers could also block an interaction between buyer and themselves. If the sub-supplier is a nexus supplier, he is probably so powerful that he does not care about the attempts by the buyer (Yan et al. 2015). Furthermore, the sub-supplier may not see the relevance of receiving help from the buyer and will refuse to receive sub-supplier specific investments.
- *Cultural Distance Between Buyer and Sub-supplier*: Just as in the dyad, cultural distance can act as a barrier to placing sub-supplier specific investments in the triad.
- *Geographical Distance Between Buyer and Sub-supplier*: As previously mentioned, it is likely that sub-suppliers will be located around the world. This increases the complexity of placing sub-supplier specific investments and could even hinder specific investments. Many sub-suppliers are located outside the buyer's country, which could be used to hold up investment in the sub-supplier. However, Shan and Hamilton (1991) found that the exchange of firm and country-specific information or knowledge results in more valuable and harder to imitate information than the exchange of information that is exchanged within one country.

Generally speaking, it can be stated that the extracted barriers must be taken into consideration when placing sub-supplier specific investments. The successful implementation of sub-supplier specific investments is dependent on being aware of potentially existing internal and external barriers. Before a buyer considers making use of sub-supplier specific investments, or sub-supplier management in general, it is necessary that he checks whether internal barriers could hinder the successful implementation. If top management support or awareness for the topic of sub-supplier management is lacking, it is unlikely that the buyer will get resources to manage his sub-supplier base. If a company is open to the topic of sub-supplier management and does not face internal barriers, the company should not forget external barriers that complicate the management of sub-suppliers.

## References

Borgatti SP, Li X (2009) On social network analysis in supply chain context. J Supply Chain Manag 45(2):5–22

Burkhardt JK (2018) Specific investments in the supply chain—a literature review on the state-of-the-art knowledge with an outlook on safeguarding mechanisms and avenues for future research. In: Bode C, Bogaschewsky R, Essig M, Lasch R, Stölzle W (eds) Supply management research: advances studies in supply management. Springer Gabler, Wiesbaden, pp 129–147

Burkhardt JK (2019) Sub-supplier management—developing lower-tier suppliers through sub-supplier specific investments. Difo-Druck, Untersiemau

Cannon JP, Achrol RS, Gundlach GT (2000) Contracts, norms and plural form governance. J Acad Mark Sci 28(2):180–194

Choi TY, Kim Y (2008) Structural embeddedness and supplier management: a network perspective. J Supply Chain Manag 44(4):5–13

Ebers M, Semrau T (2015) What drives the allocation of specific investments between buyer and supplier? J Bus Res 68(2):415–424

Hitt MA, Darcin MT, Levitas E, Arregle J-L, Borza A (2000) Partner selection in emerging and developed market contexts: resource-based and organizational learning perspective. Acad Manag Rev 26(2):264–288

Hofstetter J (2016) Towards a framework for sub-supplier management. Paper presented at the meeting of the Academy Of Management, Anaheim, CA

Hult GTM, Ketchen DJ Jr, Slater SF (2004) Information processing, knowledge development, and strategic supply chain performance. Acad Manag J 47(2):241–253

Kraljic P (1983) Purchasing must become supply management. Harv Bus Rev 61(5):109–117

Macneil I (1980) The new social contract, an inquiry into modern contractual relations. Yale University Press, New Haven, CT

Norrman A, Jansson U (2004) Ericsson's proactive supply chain risk management approach after a serious sub-supplier accident. Int J Phys Distrib Logist Manag 34(5):434–456

Rob R, Yang H (2010) Long-term relationships as safeguards. Economic Theory 43(2):143–166

Shan W, Hamilton W (1991) Country-specific advantage and international cooperation. Strateg Manag J 12:419–432

Wagner SM, Bode C (2013) Supplier relationship-specific investments and the role of safeguards for supplier innovation sharing. J Oper Manag 32(3):65–78

Williamson OE (1985) The economic institution of capitalism: firms, markets, relational contracting. Free Press, New York

Williamson OE (1991) Strategizing, economizing, and economic organization. Strateg Manag J 12:75–94

Yan T, Choi T, Kim Y, Yang Y (2015) A theory of the nexus supplier: A critical supplier from a network perspective. J Supply Chain Manag 51(1):52–66

# Sub-supplier Management and Sustainability

**Hedwig Maria Scharlipp**

**Abstract** Some of the main sustainability problems in global supply chains occur at the level of lower-tier suppliers. Focal firms may consider these issues primarily as reputational risks that should be minimized as much as possible. Sub-supplier management could be the solution, both from an ethical and a business point of view. This chapter gives insight on two questions:

1. Does sub-supplier management contribute to sustainability in supply chains?
2. For which reasons do focal firms manage their sub-suppliers, and among different reasons, which role does a firm's sustainability commitment play?

The first question is discussed in a theoretical way, while the second question is examined with a cross-sectional online survey among managers in the German-speaking area.

## 1 Introduction

Some of the main sustainability problems like environmental degradation and inhumane working conditions occur at the level of lower-tier suppliers. A study from the Wuppertal Institute about sustainability in Germany (Wuppertal Institut 2008) illustrates the problem of unsustainable resource consumption and environmental pollution in supply chains with the example of denim production. For one pair of jeans, 600 g of cotton are needed. Depending on the cultivation region, for one kilogram of cotton, up to 20,000 l of irrigation water are used. Especially in Uzbekistan and Kazakhstan, intensive cotton production resulted in the shrinking of the Aral Sea to 10% of its original size, with devastating impacts on human health and the local economy. Furthermore, subsequent processing steps as dyeing and bleaching can significantly pollute the environment. The authors of the study describe the case of the Indian textile city Tirupur, where 600 dyeing factories and

H. M. Scharlipp (✉)
ecos, Basel, Switzerland
e-mail: hedwig.scharlipp@posteo.de

© The Author(s), under exclusive license to Springer Nature Switzerland AG 2021

W. Stoelzle, J. Burkhardt (eds.), *Sub-Supplier Management*, Contributions to Management Science, https://doi.org/10.1007/978-3-030-75575-1_6

bleaching plants dumped 75,000 cubic meters of wastewater a day into the local river due to inadequate environmental regulations. Finally, a regional court condemned the local industry to compensate for the loss of agricultural yields and to take precautionary measures.

Another example that gained sad fame is the collapse of the building Rana Plaza in Bangladesh in 2013, which housed five textile factories, causing 1138 deaths. Globally renowned clothing companies have subsequently been accused of being responsible for the disaster and for the general desolate conditions in the Southeast Asian garment industry (Public Eye 2018). Because of the difficulty to identify sub-suppliers, these firms "were unable to ensure that none of their garments was produced in one of the affected factories" (Hofstetter 2016, p. 2).

While the ethical question is how to overcome such environmental problems and human rights violations in global supply chains, focal firms[1] may consider these problems primarily as reputational risks that should be minimized as much as possible, especially since NGOs tend to blame them for social and environmental misconduct throughout the supply chain (Leppelt 2014; Smith 2008; Tachizawa and Wong 2014). A well-known example is the Greenpeace campaign against deforestation and land grabbing by the Indonesian palm oil company Sinar Mas. This campaign targeted Nestlé, respectively, its KitKat brand as large purchaser of palm oil. Nestlé was required to stop the (indirect) supply relationship with Sinar Mas and to advocate the halt to deforestation towards the Indonesian government (Greenpeace-Kampagne 2010).

As the cited scandals occurred in complex global supply chains with numerous and often un-known tiers of suppliers, sub-supplier management[2] could be a solution to such sustainability problems, both from an ethical and a business point of view. However, research on sub-supplier management is still very scarce (Hofstetter 2016; Tachizawa and Wong 2014), so little is known about the reasons why focal firms decide to manage or not to manage their sub-suppliers, or whether sustainability in supply chains can be achieved through sub-supplier management practices. The following chapter therefore tries to shed light on the following two questions:

1. Does sub-supplier management contribute to sustainability in supply chains?
2. For which reasons do focal firms manage their sub-suppliers, and among different reasons, which role does a firm's sustainability commitment play?

The first question is discussed in a theoretical way, using insights from sustainable supply chain management literature as well as sustainability/CSR research. The second question is examined with a cross-sectional online survey among managers from manufacturing, wholesale, and retail firms from the German-speaking area and

[1]In line with Grimm et al. and Carter et al., the term focal firm will be used to denominate firms whose perspective is taken. Supply chains thus are relative to focal firms. A firm called sub-supplier is a sub-supplier from the perspective of some focal firm, but the same firm could be a direct supplier or a customer from a different perspective (Carter et al. 2015; Grimm et al. 2016).

[2]Defined as "the organization and coordination of a buyer's activities to achieve sub-supplier compliance with the buyer requirements" (Hofstetter 2016).

a subsequent multiple regression analysis. The aim of this chapter is to provide inspiration on how sub-supplier management practices of focal firms can contribute to improving conditions in global supply chains and on how researchers could combine a sustainability with a management perspective.

## 2 Characterization of Sustainability with Regard to Supply Chains

Sustainability is an old idea which rose to political prominence in the last few decades. The German mining administrator Hans Carl von Carlowitz is often cited as an early proponent of sustainability. In his book *Sylvicultura Oeconomica* from 1713, he teaches in response to a local timber scarcity that for forestry to be sustainable, the extraction of timber should not exceed the rate at which forests recover (Grober 2013). During the last century, however, environmental problems reached a far different, i.e., global scale. Increasing awareness for environmental pollution, resource depletion, and climate change resulted in a sequence of international conferences and the foundation of environmental organizations and programs. In the wake of this trend, the World Commission on Environment and Development (WCED) published the report "Our Common Future" (WCEP 1989) where a sustainable development is defined as a development which "[. . .] meets the needs of the present without compromising the ability of future generations to meet their own needs" (WCEP 1989, p. 16). This report is considered as the first systematic attempt to link concerns about the environment with concerns about inequality between northern and southern countries (Loske 2016). The WCED aims at overcoming the separation between environmental issues and economic development issues, as it is "[. . .] futile to attempt to deal with environmental problems without a broader perspective that encompasses the factors underlying world poverty and international inequality" (WCEP 1989, p. 12). Sustainability as new international guiding principle represented at the time of the WCED reports a paradigm shift away from traditional nature conservation where the aim is to protect nature and to minimize human impacts. In contrast to this, sustainability is future oriented and stresses the importance of development and justice. It encompasses societal and economic progress while respecting environmental limits (Burger 2015).

The difference between environmental protection and sustainability is not always understood until today. German professor and politician Reinhold Loske (2016) explains that developed countries like Germany are rightly regarded as international leaders in environmental protection. Since the industrial revolution, the quality of air and water in this country has improved significantly; even extinct species such as wolves or lynx returned. However, leadership in environmental protection should not be confounded with leadership in sustainable development. The richer a country, the higher its emissions of climate-damaging greenhouse gases, the higher its use of renewable as well as nonrenewable resources, and the higher its need for land for agricultural, mining, or industrial purposes. When it comes to greenhouse gas emissions, for example, per capita emissions in industrialized countries lie five to ten times higher than the amount with which climate change would be kept within tolerable limits[3] (Loske 2016). The resource-intensive lifestyle of the developed world's populations is in no way generalizable. For a long time, they have almost alone caused overuse of ecosystems and resources, accounting for only about one-sixth of the world's population (Wuppertal Institut 2008).

Nowadays, the term sustainability is used in an inflationary way and has been employed for various, sometimes contradictory purposes. The colloquial term "sustainable" with the meaning "durable" or "having lasting impact" must be differentiated from sustainability as an academic or political concept (Burger et al. 2011; Grober 2013). As an academic or political concept, it suffers on the one hand from countless interpretations and on the other hand from rhetorical abuse. Burger and Christen (2011) cite the controversial debate on nuclear energy, for example, where proponents as well as opponents underline their arguments by pointing to sustainability.

> Given the heterogeneity of frame conditions, sustainability might cover whatever one wishes it to cover. (Burger and Christen 2011, p. 787)

The authors therefore argue that any sustainability conception or theory must meet some basic principles in order to avoid the wholly arbitrary use of the term. However, Burger also opposes the idea of defining once and for all how a sustainable world should look like. According to him, this would be a far too strong claim considering that sustainability is concerned with the future. Future is characterized by openness and uncertainty. Too rigid a definition would be a paternalistic decision on future developments (Burger 2015). Burger and Christen (2011) formulate six adequacy conditions[4] as essential properties a sustainability conception must fulfill:

1. *Future orientation* (because of the responsibility towards future generations)
2. *Normative power and the ability to steer action* (sustainability as a normative societal guiding principle)
3. *Intra- and intergenerational justice* (a decent life for everyone)
4. *Universality* (sustainability concerns all human beings)
5. *Limited natural resources and fragile ecosystems* (respecting natural constraints as precondition for human life)
6. *Scope of action not only on individual but also on institutional/political level*

Besides these adequacy conditions, another distinction helps to judge sustainability conceptions: the distinction between strong and weak sustainability.

[3]Data about environmental threats is available, for example, on these websites: www.unep.org, www.fao.org, www.undp.org, www.eea.europa.eu/de.

[4]"Adequacy conditions contain what a theoretical concept must satisfy. They capture the object of concern and function as a basis for a critical assessment of concept A against concept B, given adequacy conditions X, Y Z (or to argue for alternative adequacy conditions)" (Burger and Christen 2011).

Advocates of strong sustainability argue that resource availability and the capacity of ecosystems are limiting factors for any form of economic or social development. If natural boundaries are exceeded systematically and permanently, irreversible damage to ecosystems and resource depletion will result. In contrast, proponents of weak sustainability operate with the model of three columns or the idea of a triangle: According to them, economic, social, and ecological goals possess equal weight and should be reconciled as much as possible (Loske 2016). Natural capital can be replaced by social or economic capital, which is not possible within the strong sustainability point of view (Aachener Stiftung Kathy Beys 2015). Critics of weak sustainability assert that future generations or non-human beings have no bargaining power over political and economic interests and are therefore likely to fall behind. They also argue that it is questionable to what extent ecological capital can effectively be replaced by social or economic capital (Loske 2016).

In the following, it is described in how far the idea of sustainability can be applied to companies as well as to supply chains. Sustainability as characterized above is a societal, macroeconomic concept. Burger and Christen as well as Loske stress the importance of a fundamental reorientation of the political framework in order to guide individuals and businesses towards more sustainable behaviors (Burger and Christen 2011; Loske 2016). For instance, carbon taxes make the use of fossil fuels more expensive while increasing the competitiveness of renewable energies, thus contributing to the diffusion of a more sustainable energy production and more sustainable transportation modes (Wuppertal Institut 2008) However, this societal, macroeconomic approach is not transferable one-to-one to individual firms. Firms may claim to pursue sustainability goals, but they must do so under existing conditions, which mainly favor non-sustainable behavior (Starmanns 2007). In addition, they must reconcile the interests of their shareholders or the requirements of capital markets with the requirements of other stakeholders such as employees or broader society and the natural environment (Carter and Rogers 2008). Conceptions of organizational sustainability like the triple bottom line (TBL) or corporate social responsibility (CSR) therefore tacitly adopt a weak sustainability point of view (Carter and Rogers 2008; Loske 2016). The idea of the TBL, which was developed in the 1990s by the English businessman and author John Elkington, explicitly uses the language of financial accounting to inspire entrepreneurs for the idea that environmental and social goals can be added to the traditional financial goals of companies (Elkington 1994). Elkington does not conceal that these three areas are partly in conflict and that a profound paradigm change in corporate culture and practice as well as a change of the political framework is needed in order to reach corporate sustainability (Jeurissen 2000). But Elkington can as well be seen as one prominent proponent of the idea of a win-win-win-situation in which the pursuit of social and environmental goals serves to increase competitiveness and create profit (Carter and Rogers 2008). On the one hand, this shift towards economic goals in the target dimensions of sustainability allowed entrepreneurs to sympathize with the idea of sustainability. On the other hand, "[e]nvironmental and social activities which can harm or at least not help the economic bottom line [. . .]" (Carter and Rogers 2008) cannot be called sustainable anymore. Moreover, the idea of sustainability has been distorted and diluted to the point that any company can claim to be sustainable without addressing the slightest change in its culture or practice, a development known as "green washing" (Sarkis et al. 2011).

Pagell and Wu's distinction between three different trajectories helps to shed light on how sustainability can be "operationalized/introduced into the supply chain and how the series of decisions managers make will, overtime, determine how/if true sustainability would develop in that specific supply chain" (Pagell and Wu 2017). The authors define a truly sustainable supply chain as a supply chain which "would at a minimum create no harm and might even have positive or regenerative impacts on social and environmental systems while maintaining economic viability" (Pagell and Wu 2017). They distinguish the balanced, the focused, and the opportunity-first trajectory. The balanced trajectory means that firms decide to dedicate equal importance to environmental, social, and economic goals in their supply chains. In the short term, this will increase costs, but in the long run, viable, stable, and innovative business models can emerge, enabling the enterprise to operate for very long periods of time. They describe the example of The Collins Companies, a US wood processing enterprise that invests heavily in sustainable forestry, eco-efficiency, its workforce, and surrounding communities. Apart from the fact that Collins will not deplete its resources and that they benefit from a very positive reputation, this trajectory creates constraints in the form of inflexibility as well. Collins cannot respond to a sudden increase in demand, i.e., their growth is limited.

Firms on a focused trajectory in turn decide to focus either on environmental protection or on social goals. As a consequence, they develop a competitive advantage out of innovative practices and a clear profile in the chosen area but lag behind in the dimension they chose to neglect. The social or environmental motive is the cause of their business, so that profitability is no longer an end in itself but a means of achieving social or environmental goals.

The opportunity-first trajectory is described as the most common but also the riskiest trajectory. Here, companies primarily start to engage in sustainability initiatives for reasons of profit, e.g., by adopting eco-efficiency measures for cost reduction or social initiatives for a better reputation. Companies on an opportunity-first trajectory are better known by consumers for their low prices than for their sustainability commitment. They therefore face the problem that it will be difficult to charge price premiums for higher environmental or social quality. If no substantive action is taken on sustainability claims, they also risk serious reputation problems (Pagell and Wu 2017).

The distinction of different trajectories makes clear that the adoption of sustainability goals and practices by firms happens in various different ways, relative to a firm's history and its overall strategic positioning. Sustainability in supply chains can therefore on the one hand be characterized as a guiding principle with utopian character and on the other hand as a bunch of practices which result from different motives and which are more or less far from the ideal of true sustainability. Bouchery et al. sum up this tension between ideal and reality by stating that we should not talk about sustainable supply chains, but rather about the "[...] Gradual but Never-Ending Paths Towards Less Unsustainable Global Value Networks" (Bouchery et al. 2017, p. 3). Their definition of supply chain sustainability reflects a humble approach in the face of numerous practical constraints and difficulties: "[. . .] a more sustainable supply chain is one that is better at identifying current and future environmental and social impacts and finding ways to mitigate those" (Bouchery et al. 2017).

Following the previous considerations, sustainability in supply chains will be defined in this thesis adopting two different angles: First, there is the organizational perspective adopted by individual companies targeting the introduction of sustainable SCM practices for a variety of reasons. Second, there is a societal point of view in which sustainable supply chains are mandatory in order to achieve the goal of intra- and intergenerational justice while respecting the limits of nature.

The organizational perspective is covered by a definition of sustainable SCM (SSCM) from Carter and Rogers. They define SSCM "[. . .] as the strategic, transparent integration and achievement of an organization's social, environmental, and economic goals in the systemic coordination of key interorganizational business processes for improving the long-term economic performance of the individual company and its supply chains" (Carter and Rogers 2008, p. 368). Carter and Roger's definition clarifies that organizations must first and foremost ensure their own survival before pursuing social and environmental goals. But they also emphasize that securing economic performance should be long term, which is a clear call against short-term profit maximization. However, their definition must be clearly complemented by a definition of sustainable supply chains from a societal point of view, as it remains totally unclear what exactly the social and environmental goals of an organization could be with regard to the supply chain.

For this purpose, the characterization of eco-fair value chains by Starmanns (2007) is used. The author speaks of value chains rather than supply chains because, according to him, the consumption and disposal phases of products must be taken into account in order to assess their full environmental and social impact. Even from a purely organizational point of view, this extension is relevant in that firms may influence these downstream phases by product design, recycling, and return programs.

Eco-fair value chains

> [. . .] maintain and promote the viability and diversity of ecosystems and their functions in the long term by preventing or reducing damage. Those who cause unavoidable damage are obliged to compensate for it. Furthermore, they offer participants and affected parties alike the possibility of social and economic participation. This means that everyone has the opportunity to improve her own position, e.g. by suing for rights and participating in the value creation process, and to shape her own life with her own hands. Finally, eco-fair value chains promote the betterment of the least favored by helping to reduce poverty and secure basic needs. (Starmanns 2007, p. 13)

Starmanns substantiates this definition with four guiding principles:

1. Eco-fair value chains aim at ensuring quality in a comprehensive sense: Besides product quality, the environmental and social quality of production and transportation processes must be guaranteed. Internationally agreed standards like the

Declaration on Fundamental Principles and Rights at Work by the ILO or the Convention on Biological Diversity should apply to the whole value chain.
2. Eco-fair value chains result in prices that reflect the internalization of all environmental and social costs. Living wages along the supply chain are part of this.
3. Eco-fair value chains offer long-term development opportunities to all their participants. This happens on the basis of long-term collaborative cooperation between supply chain members. Interests of weaker partners are included in decision processes, and more powerful partners assume a larger share of responsibilities for an eco-fair value creation according to their higher capacities.
4. Eco-fair value chains need political frameworks which secure the limits within which economic activities must happen. These frameworks imply principles of intra- and intergenerational justice and the recognition of the maximum capacity and resilience of ecosystems.

The above definition and the four guiding principles provide a good guide for firms on what their environmental and social goals might be. However, they clearly go beyond the horizons of individual firms, as they cannot be realized on an organizational level alone. As elaborated in principle four, in order to achieve truly eco-fair supply chains, a fundamental change in political frameworks must strengthen firms' sustainability commitments and impede unsustainable practices.

## 3 Relevance of Sub-supplier Management for Sustainable Supply Chains

The relevance of sub-supplier management (SSM) for sustainable supply chains is not easily judged. SSM encompasses a whole variety of different practices (Hofstetter 2016; Tachizawa and Wong 2014). Each type of practice may have different impacts on the sustainability of the supply chain. Moreover, focal firms possibly introduce SSM practices due to various strategic motivations. The question of whether SSM resulting from a sustainability commitment of a focal firm leads to an "increase of sub-suppliers' compliance with corporate sustainability standards" (Grimm et al. 2016) has at least received some attention. The question in how far SSM resulting from other strategic motivations affects supply chain sustainability has not even been raised. In addition, while some SSM practices possibly tend to influence social issues, others may be more likely to affect environmental issues. This makes the overall evaluation of SSM with regard to sustainability—understood as multifaceted concept with a social, an environmental, and an economic dimension—even more difficult. Finally, different industries likely exhibit different constellations with regard to supply chain structure, power relations, product characteristics, sustainability challenges, and stakeholder attention, among other aspects. In view of this complex situation, a general judgment on the relevance of SSM for supply chain sustainability is only of limited validity. It definitively has to be adapted to each specific constellation of the abovementioned aspects (type of SSM, goal of SSM, sustainability dimension, and industry).

As mentioned above, some of the main sustainability problems like environmental degradation or inhumane working conditions occur at the level of lower-tier suppliers. The SSM literature as well as NGOs like the Clean Clothes Campaign or Oxfam mainly focuses on sustainability problems within the food and the garment industry (Clean Clothes Campaign 2005; Grimm et al. 2014; Mena et al. 2013; Wilshaw 2010). But poor working conditions and environmental degradation occur in other industries as well, as has been documented, for example, by Klaus Werner-Lobo and Hans Weiss for more than 300 globally known brands from a variety of sectors (Werner-Lobo and Weiss 2006). In a very general sense, SSM may contribute to the mitigation of sustainability problems in global supply chains, because it addresses the level at which the worst sustainability problems occur (Tachizawa and Wong 2014). However, this simple assumption will be questioned in the following.

Private standards or certification systems, either set by the focal firm itself or by third parties like, for example, multi-stakeholder initiatives, are an important part of SSM (Grimm et al. 2016; Hofstetter 2016; Tachizawa and Wong 2014). The critical assessment of standards by researchers and NGOs can thus give some insight about the relationship between SSM and sustainability.

Critical voices describe the impact of standards, especially in the food and the clothing industry, as superficial at best and at worst as contributing to even greater social injustice and the misleading of consumers. In March 2018 a German newspaper reported on how the market power of the four largest German food retailers negatively affects suppliers and sub-suppliers. These food retailers are said to exercise their market power not only by dictating prices but also by increasingly demanding compliance with sustainability and quality standards from suppliers and sub-suppliers. Certification costs are passed on to a large extent to food processing companies and farmers who complain that they are crushed between low margins and high-quality and sustainability requirements. Bankruptcies are the result (Grefe and Zimmermann 2018). The same negative interplay between market power and so-called ethical trading standards has been observed in the British food industry. Fox and Vorley find evidence that "when supermarkets do adopt instruments of self-regulation and CSR, such as codes of conduct on labour standards or environmental issues, the associated costs and risks can be passed up the chain as an 'unfunded mandate', resulting in a disproportional allocation of costs and benefits between standards 'makers' and standards 'takers'" (Fox and Vorley 2004). According to Fuchs et al., quality and safety standards in the food sector create additional constraints with regard to market access especially for small producers and farmers in the Global South.[5] The required investments to achieve compliance with these

[5]"Global South" is a term for economically disadvantaged geographical regions and is used as a more neutral alternative to terms such as "third world" or "developing countries." It encompasses as well poor and marginalized parts of the population in northern countries; thus the term "South" has a geographical as well as a political connotation (Garland Mahler 2017).

standards often are not affordable for them (Fuchs et al. 2011). Consequently, standards, at least as reported for the food sector, threat to increase existing injustice and widen the gap between powerful actors from the Global Nord and poor sub-suppliers from the Global South, but also among different actors within industrialized countries like Germany or the UK.

Additionally, Oxfam and the Clean Clothes Campaign (CCC) criticize that the widespread establishment of social audits in the garment and the food industry only rarely leads to substantial amelioration of working conditions upstream in supply chains. Apart from offloading the cost of compliance onto suppliers respectively sub-suppliers, standards and the associated audits risk to provide false evidence because of fraud and corruption. Moreover, corrective actions focus mainly on health and safety issues, which are secondary to workers' views, when they suffer from starvation wages, excessive overtime, missing contracts, and the prohibition of trade unions (Clean Clothes Campaign 2005; Wilshaw 2010). The CCC underlines that internal or company monitoring and independent verification by third-party auditors must be differentiated, the latter possibly leading to higher transparency. In addition, standards set by multi-stakeholder initiatives are said to be more stringent than standards set by private companies, because NGOs and other stakeholders from the civil society have a say there. Nevertheless, the CCC fears that the practice of social auditing programs promotes above all "[. . .] a 'lowering of the bar', in order to make it easier to tell consumers that they [clothing retailers] are meeting goals for treating workers responsibly" (Clean Clothes Campaign 2005).

Similar critiques have been uttered with regard to environmental management standards, like, for example, ISO 14001. Terlaak found empirical evidence for a sample of 5215 US manufacturing facilities that "plants with poorer environmental performance (relative to other industry plants) are more likely to certify with ISO 14001" (Terlaak 2007). Social as well as environmental standards therefore cannot simply be trusted as indicators neither for superior social or environmental performance nor for efforts to improve the same. Rather, there is the tendency that they exclusively serve focal firms by providing "the benefit of appearing green (leading to legitimacy) without requiring many effective and costly actions" (Seele and Gatti 2015).

Besides the potential misleading of consumers and business partners, social and environmental certification schemes and the associated lobbying of firms carry the risk of preventing stricter environmental or social laws and regulations (Wuppertal Institut 2008).

In order to distinguish between greenwashing and genuine sustainability commitments of firms in supply chains, the critical literature on standards and multi-stakeholder initiatives proposes to apply criteria of democratic legitimacy like participation, transparency, and accountability to phenomena summarized under the term "private governance" (Fuchs et al. 2011; Schaller 2007; Starmanns 2007). These criteria of democratic legitimacy build on constitutional, pluralistic, and deliberative democracy theory and were originally formulated by Klaus Dingwerth (Schaller 2007). Participation means that all affected parties (stakeholders) of a governance mechanism should have equal opportunity to participate in decision-making processes, so that their concerns are considered. In particular, the participation of disadvantaged groups should be ensured. For instance, representatives of factory workers should be integrated in the organizational structure of a certification institution, as this is the case in the Fair Wear Foundation (Starmanns 2007). If the idea of sustainability is to be taken seriously, participation should even be extended to those who are least able to express themselves: non-human beings and future generations. Since, of course, they cannot participate themselves, they would somehow have to be represented, e.g., by environmental or other NGOs (Dobson 1996).

Transparency is needed as prerequisite for participation and critical verification and comprises "[. . .] the provision of timely, reliable and comprehensible information on the governance and performance characteristics of standards" (Fuchs et al. 2011). According to the CCC, social audits lack credibility as long as auditing methods and reports are kept secret and garment companies do not publish information about the composition and conditions of their supply chains, or about who pays for the audits or who is the auditor (Clean Clothes Campaign 2005).

Finally, accountability means that there exist mechanisms by which affected persons can hold decision-makers accountable such that they are able to vote them out of office if they act against the affected persons' interests (Fuchs et al. 2011). Transparency again is an important prerequisite, as, for instance, workers must know about their rights or about existing complaint mechanisms.

Overall, participation, transparency, and accountability are important criteria for assessing whether standards or other SSM practices contribute to a sustainable development in supply chains. If participation, transparency, and accountability are realized in SSM, chances are high that the interests of less influential or disadvantaged stakeholders will be taken into account, ensuring both intergenerational and intragenerational equity.

An additional criterion in order to judge if specific SSM practices serve to enhance the sustainability of supply chains is the question if they contribute to long-term collaboration between focal firms, suppliers, and sub-suppliers or not. Long-term collaboration may on the one hand lead to a more effective implementation of environmental or social goals (if these exist) by better communication, mutual understanding, the transfer of knowledge, and resource sharing (Bowen et al. 2001). On the other hand, there is the possibility that long-term partnerships with suppliers and sub-suppliers constitute a counter development to "the short-termism of the competitive market economy that prevents attention to the degradation of the natural environment" (Preuss 2005), thus contributing to more sustainability in supply chains. For example, Oxfam explains how the nature of the relationship of a buying company to its suppliers determines working conditions of suppliers or sub-suppliers. If purchasing practices involve frequent changes to specifications and aggressive price negotiations, suppliers and sub-suppliers will be under time and cost pressure, ultimately straining workers due to high performance targets, low wages, excessive overtime, or harsh treatment. A better relationship with suppliers and sub-suppliers could help to prevent such problems, e.g., by using longer-term contracts and better forecasting. For genuine improvements, cost and lead time

**Table 1** Participants per country (prior to data cleansing)

| Country | No. of participants | Percentage of participants (%) |
|---|---|---|
| Austria | 8 | 5.75 |
| Belgium | 1 | 0.72 |
| Germany | 57 | 41.01 |
| Liechtenstein | 1 | 0.72 |
| Switzerland | 94 | 67.63 |

Source: Authors' own table

requirements of focal firms should not be entirely in conflict with their quality and sustainability commitments (Wilshaw 2010).

Such long-term relationships among supply chain members and possibly related ameliorations of employment conditions could result from SSM practices regardless of their goal. More precisely, even if the aim of SSM is not the compliance with sustainability standards but, for example, quality improvements or risk prevention, workers at production sites in the Global South could benefit indirectly.

There are multiple SSM practices, different conditions depending on the respective industry, possibly a variety of reasons for the implementation of SSM practices, and finally the whole complexity of the sustainability concept. A general statement about the relevance of SSM for sustainable supply chains is therefore not possible; differentiated assessments of specific constellations are required. Criteria such as participation, transparency, accountability, and long-term collaboration may help to assess specific initiatives. Whether activities at the enterprise or supply chain level ultimately lead to a development that is sustainable on a global scale, of course, also depends on consumer behavior and national and international laws and regulations.

## 4 Empirical Investigation of Reasons for Sub-supplier Management: Research Methodology

As part of a research project at the Institute of Supply Chain Management of the University of St. Gallen, a cross-sectional online survey was carried out in May and June 2018. The following section shortly explains its methodology.

The aim of the survey was to find out for which reasons firms manage their sub-suppliers. The survey was targeted at managers or owners from firms of the German-speaking area for which SSM is—theoretically—relevant, that is, manufacturing, wholesale, and retail firms. Service firms are assumed not to have sub-suppliers; hence they were not part of the target population.

Participants were recruited via voluntary and convenience sampling. 161 of 1375 contacted persons completed the survey (response rate 11.71%). Data cleaning was carried out by verifying if the response time lied in a reasonable range. Respondents with less than 8 min response time were deleted. Data cleaning resulted in a final sample of 141 participants (Table 1).

The questionnaire was established according to the following logical structure, serving as basis for the subsequent multiple regression analysis: As Schnell, Hill, and Esser (2013) point out, a questionnaire should not contain questions asking simply for reasons, as the respondents may not even be aware of the reasons themselves. Rather, questions should be designed such that background information can be obtained without asking respondents directly for justifications. According to the authors, the identification of reasons is essentially part of the analysis phase and should not be the task of the respondents. Hence, reasons why firms decide to manage or not to manage their sub-suppliers are revealed by identifying and empirically testing both positive and negative determinants of SSM adoption by firms. These determinants figure as independent variables, whereas the measurement of the existence respectively the extent of SSM represents the dependent variable. Both types of variables will be explained in the following. A causal relationship is assumed between the determinants and the existence and extent of SSM, such that changes in these determinants precede and induce changes in the extent of SSM (Weiber and Mühlhaus 2014). After data collection, multiple regression analysis was used to estimate which determinants effectively have a positive or negative effect on the existence respectively the extent of SSM practices of the sampled firms.

Reasons for SSM were operationalized based on SSM literature as two sets of determinants: on the one hand, so-called strategic orientations that capture corporate strategies, for example, in relation to reputation, sustainability, quality, or innovation and on the other hand contextual factors such as firm size, legal form, industry, or dependency on suppliers (see Table 2 for an overview about these variables and the related survey items). Strategic orientations were surveyed with variable X1–X7 and contextual factors with variable X8–X15.

Variables X1–X7 and X10–X12 are operationalized as multi-item scales. Multi-item scales are used to measure concepts that cannot be directly observed, called hypothetical constructs or latent variables. By using several items to measure the hypothetical construct, possible distortions because of differing understandings of each item among respondents can be compensated. Items in this survey consisted of statements that participants had to evaluate with regard to the situation in their firm. Answer options ranged from 1 = strongly disagree to 5 = strongly agree. The resulting scores were aggregated into so-called factor scores using principal component factor analysis.

Besides the reasons for SSM, the existence respectively the extent of SSM was measured in the survey. For this purpose, a list of 22 SSM practices was derived from SSM literature (see Table 3). For each practice, respondents were asked to indicate whether their firm carries out the practice, giving the following choice of responses: (1) *carried out*, (2) *planned*, (3) *not carried out but could be considered*, and (4) *not carried out and probably not considered*. The distinction of four answer options was made in order to reduce the risk of socially desirable responding. Bowen et al. (2001) found in a pretest with a similar answer scale that the middle category "planned" reduced the inclination of respondents to claim that they carry out a certain activity when they were only planning it, or not to respond at all, rather than to admit that they have not implemented it. The distinction between (3) and

**Table 2** Determinants of SSM and survey items

| Variable | Survey items |
|---|---|
| X1: Reputation orientation | 1. It is important for us to be able to prevent sub-suppliers from damaging our image<br>2. It is important for us to be able to prevent suppliers from damaging our image<br>3. It is important for us to strengthen our image as a responsible company<br>4. It is important for us to communicate comprehensively about our sustainability or CSR activities<br>5. It is important for us to make our supply chain transparent to our consumers and other stakeholders<br>6. Reporting on sustainability and CSR activities is very important to my company |
| X2: Sustainability orientation | 1. It is important for us to be able to ensure that our sustainability standards are met in the supply chain<br>2. It is important for us to consider and involve our stakeholders<br>3. We always attempt to go beyond basic compliance with laws and regulations on environmental and social issues<br>4. Sustainability is an integral part of our corporate philosophy<br>5. Sustainability, CSR, and environmental protection: These or similar values do not only exist on paper but are lived in everyday business<br>6. Our corporate management places a high priority on sustainability |
| X3: Risk management orientation | 1. It is important for us to understand and reduce risks in the supply chain<br>2. The stability of supplier relationships is very important in my company<br>3. My company has a strong awareness of supply chain risks |
| X4: Quality orientation | 1. It is important for us to offer our customers outstanding quality<br>2. It is important for us to ensure that quality standards are met in the supply chain<br>3. The quality of our products is an important unique selling point |
| X5: Delivery performance orientation | 1. It is important for us to minimize delivery failures<br>2. It is important for us that suppliers react quickly and reliably to change requests<br>3. It is important for us that suppliers deliver on time |
| X6: Cost reduction orientation | 1. It is important for us to reduce purchasing costs<br>2. It is important for us to increase cost efficiency in the supply chain<br>3. It is important for us to use resources efficiently in order to minimize costs |
| X7: Innovation orientation | 1. It is important for us to recognize new market trends at an early stage<br>2. Openness to new ideas is part of our corporate culture |

(continued)

**Table 2** (continued)

| Variable | Survey items |
|---|---|
| | 3. In my company, great importance is attached to collecting, integrating, and applying new knowledge |
| X8: Firm size | Please indicate the number of employees in your company |
| X9: Legal form | Please tick the legal form of your company |
| X10: Public visibility | 1. My company has brands with a high degree of recognition<br>2. My company is attracting media attention<br>3. End users are interested in my company<br>4. My company is known to the public |
| X11: Channel power | 1. Our suppliers are dependent on my company as a customer<br>2. My company has a strong negotiating position with our suppliers<br>3. Our suppliers have a strong interest in meeting our requirements<br>4. If our suppliers do not meet our requirements, my company may impose sanctions |
| X12: Dependency on suppliers | 1. We are heavily dependent on our suppliers<br>2. My company has difficulties changing suppliers<br>3. It is very time-consuming to switch to new suppliers<br>4. It is very expensive to switch to new suppliers<br>5. If our suppliers perform poorly, we perform poorly as well |
| X13: Sustainability-oriented turnover share (SOTS) | 1. Does your company advertise products with the following (or similar) terms? "green," "sustainable," "organic," "environmentally friendly," "fair"<br>2. What is the estimated share of sales generated by your company with products that are advertised with the terms "green," "sustainable," "organic," "environmentally friendly," "fair," or similar? |
| X14: Industry | Please indicate the main industry of your company |
| X15: Supplier distance | Please indicate how the purchasing volume of your company is distributed over the following three regions of origin: national, European foreign countries, and non-European foreign countries |

Source: Authors' own table

(4) allows to observe the degree of interest in SSM practices even if in a firm they are neither carried out nor planned. The distinction between (1) and (2) moreover allows to take into account a greater variance in the extent of SSM, as the planning of SSM practices can be considered as part of the management process. Hence, the existence of SSM is measured with answer options (1) and (2) and the extent with the number of practices per respondents within the categories (1) and (2). In summary, the dependent variable is operationalized as additive index with multiple items measured on an ordinal answer scale.

**Table 3** List of SSM practices

| Variable | SSM practice |
|---|---|
| Y1–1 | Identification of relevant sub-suppliers, e.g., as part of supply chain mapping |
| Y1–2 | Evaluation/classification of relevant sub-suppliers as part of a risk analysis |
| Y1–3 | Requirement towards suppliers that sub-suppliers must comply with certain standards, e.g., codes of conduct |
| Y1–4 | Selection of new sub-suppliers with the help of suppliers |
| Y1–5 | Selection of new sub-suppliers by your firm |
| Y1–6 | Introduction of new sub-suppliers with the help of suppliers |
| Y1–7 | Introduction of new sub-suppliers by your firm |
| Y1–8 | Requirement of self-assessments from sub-suppliers |
| Y1–9 | Site visits to sub-suppliers |
| Y1–10 | Formal audits conducted by your firm |
| Y1–11 | Formal audits conducted by third parties |
| Y1–12 | Trainings/workshops for sub-suppliers by your firm |
| Y1–13 | Trainings/workshops for sub-suppliers by third parties |
| Y1–14 | Coordination with sub-suppliers with regard to specific elements of the corporate strategy |
| Y1–15 | Collaboration with sub-suppliers in terms of research |
| Y1–16 | Collaboration with sub-suppliers in terms of product development |
| Y1–17 | Financial support of sub-suppliers |
| Y1–18 | Sub-supplier procurement support |
| Y1–19 | Purchasing contracts with sub-suppliers ("directed sourcing") |
| Y1–20 | Sub-supplier phaseout with the help of suppliers |
| Y1–21 | Sub-supplier phaseout by your firm |
| Y1–22 | Influencing the environment of sub-suppliers, e.g., through stakeholder alliances, lobbying, industry associations, NGOs, or similar |

Source: Authors' own table

## 5 Empirical Investigation of Reasons for Sub-supplier Management: Results

To the author's best knowledge, this is the first study examining determinants for sub-supplier management in a cross-sectional survey. It can be stated that focal firms manage their sub-suppliers because of a strategic orientation on reputation, risk management, quality, and innovation. If a sustainability commitment is one of the reasons for the introduction and expansion of SSM, however, this effect is weak. A strategic orientation on sustainability can at most be considered as determinant of SSM which plays a subordinate role.

Moreover, sub-suppliers are more likely to be managed if focal firms are large, if they strongly depend on their suppliers, and if sourcing is geared primarily to European rather than national or non-European suppliers. Larger firms and firms which are more dependent on suppliers adopt more SSM practices.

However, if focal firms possess a strategic orientation on cost reduction and on delivery performance, they are less likely to manage their sub-suppliers, and if they manage them, they adopt fewer SSM practices.

Focal firms with a higher public visibility are less likely to adopt SSM in the first place. Yet, this effect is weak and should not be overinterpreted.

The following paragraphs elaborate on the implications of these results. First of all, as presumed, for example, by Grimm et al. (2014) and Tachizawa and Wong (2014), a sustainability commitment as primary or important reason for focal firms to engage in SSM could not be confirmed. A more salient reason for SSM is a reputation orientation. As the reputation and the sustainability orientation variable highly correlate, a firm's sustainability commitment and the motivation to avoid reputation problems, respectively, to gain a positive image seem to be closely intertwined. It is in no firm's interest to admit that its sustainability commitment is mainly based on reputation concerns, as this would undermine the positive effect on the image (Eisenegger and Schranz 2011). Moreover, a sustainability commitment based on altruistic rather than instrumental motives most likely has a positive effect on a firm's reputation. Not exploiting this effect and gaining competitive advantage from it would be simply unreasonable, especially as higher cost from sustainable management activities need to be balanced by charging higher prices (Peters and Zelewski 2013; Smith 2008). It is therefore probably easy to confound both types of motivations in case studies, or to just pass over it. A statement from a participant especially well illustrates this close relationship between sustainability and reputation orientation:

> Every year, we have our activities in the areas of risk management, sustainability and supplier management measured externally. It is important for us to appear in the Dow Jones Sustainability Index as a leader in our industry. (Participant no. 44)

Fittingly, this participant shows the maximum rate of approval with regard to both the sustainability and the reputation orientation scale. Furthermore, the cited participant achieves nearly the maximum value in the dependent variable, that is, his firm carries out nearly all of the 22 listed SSM practices.

A reputation/sustainability orientation is one reason for focal firms to manage sub-suppliers, among others. A quality orientation and an innovation orientation seem to be the most important motivations, along with risk management, which, however, is only a significant determinant in one of two regression models. Multicollinearity and, more precisely, the correlation between risk management and innovation orientation are possible reasons why it is difficult to separately account for the effect of a risk management orientation. In addition, a risk management orientation overlaps with other strategic orientations. It can even be called a cross-sectional motivation, as it permeates areas like reputation, sustainability, quality, delivery performance, and cost likewise. The relatively frequent mention of risk management activities in response to the open question about further SSM practices in the questionnaire can be taken as an indication that this aspect has probably been underrepresented in the dependent variable. So, it seems reasonable to assume that a risk management orientation is at least as important than a quality and an innovation orientation.

Quality is mentioned as one of the core competitive priorities of purchasing (Krause et al. 2001) and as one of the most important supplier selection criteria (Vonderembse and Tracey 1999). In a survey among Indian small and medium enterprises, "quality improvement" turns out to be the first priority in supply chain management strategies (Kumar et al. 2014). Innovation as well figures among the core competitive priorities of purchasing: "Companies in industries where quality and cost are order-qualifiers, may try to compete through innovation of new products and/or processes in order to differentiate themselves from their low-cost, high-quality competitors" (Krause et al. 2001). Moreover, there is strong empirical evidence that product and process innovation improve the long-run economic performance of firms (McWilliams and Siegel 2000). The clear evidence that a quality and an innovation orientation are reasons for focal firms to manage their sub-suppliers is not surprising in this regard.

Two theoretical angles underline the prevalence of the reputation, the quality, the risk management, and the innovation orientation as determinants for SSM compared to a sustainability orientation. First, with recourse to Michael E. Porter's (1989) well-established distinction between the generic competitive strategies of cost leadership and differentiation, these four strategic orientations can be understood as part of a differentiation strategy of a firm. This strategy consists in a firm's attempt to be unique in its industry with regard to some dimensions that are valued by its customers. It tries to develop a distinctive position in the chosen dimensions and aims at a price premium that offsets the additional cost (Porter 1989). SSM in order to assure extraordinary quality standards, to tap "[. . .] into suppliers' creativity for product and process improvements" (Choi and Krause 2006), to proactively address all sorts of supply chain risks, and, finally, to secure an excellent reputation by taking a pioneer position with regard to ethical issues absolutely makes sense in the light of the differentiation strategy. Investments into SSM pay off if they contribute to the establishment of a long-term competitive advantage.

The other theoretical angle is represented by Starmanns (2007) who argues that in the light of institutional theory, organizations react to pressures from stakeholders as they aim at being perceived as socially legitimated agents. Interests of more powerful or more relevant stakeholders are accordingly of primary concern: the willingness of focal firms to assume responsibility, e.g., for the amelioration of working conditions at sub-supplier production sites, ends when it conflicts with the interests of customers or investors (Starmanns 2007).

Both theoretical angles are explanations why a reputation, a quality, a risk management, and an innovation orientation prevail as determinants of SSM, whereas a sustainability orientation plays a subordinate role.

Contrary to Hofstetter's (2016) assumption that the objectives of SSM correspond to those of supplier management, cost reduction and delivery performance are reasons for focal firms not to engage with sub-suppliers. This finding can be supported by several arguments.

A cost reduction orientation can have different sources. First, it corresponds to Porter's other generic competitive strategy called cost leadership. This strategy consists in a firm's aim to become the most cost-effective manufacturer in the industry. It implies that all sources of cost advantages must be identified and used and that prices can be pushed through which translate the cost advantage into high revenues. A firm which pursues this competitive strategy must try to be the one with the lowest cost in the market, because a struggle between several competitors for cost leadership can be detrimental for the whole industry (Porter 1989). What does a cost leadership strategy entail with regard to SSM? The adoption of SSM practices is not compatible with this strategy, since competitors who do not engage in SSM will realize lower cost by neglecting SSM. A cost leadership strategy therefore might prevent that focal firms adopt SSM practices, or it might limit their SSM efforts to the most necessary minimum.

Second, a cost reduction strategy may stem from a disadvantaged position which results from a lack of resources. For focal firms in such a situation, SSM simply is not affordable. Initial investments and current costs are too high compared to benefits which are uncertain and can potentially be realized only in the long run. Reasons why SSM is unprofitable are manifold; among others they comprise low margins (Smith 2008), a high number of sub-suppliers and dynamic sourcing markets, distance to sub-suppliers, non-cooperative behavior of suppliers, or a lack of power in the supply chain (Grimm et al. 2014; Hofstetter 2016). The following statement from a survey participant exemplifies such a situation:

> Our purchasing volume is spread over so many products and countries of origin that we are dependent on our suppliers and, above all, the certificates accompanying the goods. It is impossible for us (financially/with regard to the effort) to audit every sub-supplier ourselves. We buy natural products and are therefore dependent on crop yields. If there are problems, we have to find other sources and change supplier and/or sub-supplier. The regulations concerning sub-supplier management in our sector are becoming stricter every day and we as Swiss company with a small market and therefore small purchasing volume can soon no longer participate, as the costs for the entire quality and sub-supplier management have to be spread over much smaller quantities than, for example, with a German processor. It seems as if the time of the small or medium sized companies is over!! (Participant no. 393)

The explanation why a delivery performance orientation is a negative determinant of SSM is a bit less straightforward. Delivery performance or supply responsiveness could be enhanced by a closer collaboration among supply chain partners; therefore, a positive correlation between a delivery performance orientation and SSM was hypothesized in the study. A possible explanation for the finding contrary to the initial hypothesis is that mainly respondents from firms without a professional supply chain management approach showed high levels of approval towards this strategic orientation (keeping in mind that nearly every respondent approved this strategic orientation). In the absence of an elaborated SCM strategy, purchasing is likely to be exercised from "[. . .] a routine clerical perspective concerned with little more than purchase price and continuity of supply" (Preuss 2005). As a large gap between the theoretical ideal of strategic cooperation along the ultimate supply chain and business practice has been identified (Fawcett and Magnan 2002), possibly a significant number of focal firms with a rather traditional and narrow perception of SCM exist. These companies focus primarily on cost reduction and material availability, leaving issues with sub-suppliers to their direct suppliers. Grimm et al. (2014) assert that supply know-how of focal firms is a prerequisite for the management of sub-suppliers, in order to cope with higher levels of complexity compared with the management of direct suppliers.

In summary, a cost leadership strategy and a lack of financial resources or of supply know-how are considered as underlying reasons why a cost reduction and a delivery performance orientation turned out to be negative determinants of SSM. In turn, the finding that a reputation, quality, risk management, and innovation orientation and, perhaps, to a limited extent a sustainability commitment are positive determinants of SSM is attributed to a competitive strategy of differentiation and the response to pressure from powerful stakeholders.

Two contextual factors proved to be crucial as determinants for SSM: firm size and dependency on suppliers. Firm size was significant in most specifications of regression analysis, but not in all. It is impossible to explain all technical details here, but this result leads to the presumption that firm size is an enabling factor rather with regard to the expansion of SSM and less with regard to the adoption of first SSM practices. That makes sense insofar as firm size is linked to economies of scale. Large firms possess stronger cash flows to fund investments into SSM. They have a larger volume of sales and therefore are able to spread the fixed cost of SSM over a larger sales base. Moreover, they possibly have better access to knowledge and skilled employees than small firms. A lack of expertise and functional specialization could be a reason why SSM is less considered in small firms. They could be less aware of opportunities as well as risks from beyond the direct commercial relationships (Rogers 2004). Additionally, firm size could control for a variety of unobserved contextual factors as the regulatory environment, different levels of risk due to the number of products and supply chain complexity, different levels of institutional or NGO pressure, and critical observation by the media.

The contextual variable *dependency on suppliers* interestingly is among the variables with the most stable positive impact on the existence and extent of SSM. Its operationalization is very similar to the dependency construct of Awaysheh and Klassen (2010), who in contrast did not find evidence that dependency on suppliers (negatively!) affects the adoption of supplier responsible practices (e.g., supplier human rights, supplier labor practices). Supplier responsible practices have some commonalities but as well differences with SSM practices, so a different logic most likely is valid in our case. Whereas supplier responsible practices are directed at direct suppliers, SSM is directed at sub-suppliers. SSM comprises practices like site visits or audits which require direct interaction with suppliers and/or sub-suppliers as well as practices where direct interaction is not necessary, e.g., supply chain mapping. Furthermore, goals of SSM are probably more varied than the goals of supplier responsible practices. Therefore, it can be concluded that SSM is not hindered by the dependency on suppliers, but rather encouraged, as it is a means to cope with a lack of power in face of monopolistic situations on supply markets or because of the non-substitutability of specific materials or components. A comment by a survey participant underlines this relationship:

> The interest in knowing the sub-supplier is very strongly related to the product group to be procured. (Participant no. 284)

Supplier responsible practices may depend on the collaboration of suppliers, whereas SSM, at least internal SSM, can be carried out without the contribution of suppliers or sub-suppliers. Supplier responsible practices may be mainly motivated by a sustainability or a reputation orientation, whereas SSM is carried out because of a variety of different goals. The urgency to act is highest if stakes are high; this is the case if a firm is dependent on suppliers. The variable *dependency on suppliers* might as well reflect the degree to which a focal firm generally relies on purchased material and components, i.e., if its vertical integration is low. In that case, dependency on suppliers would be present just because of high expenditures on sourced material, even without any problematic situation on sourcing markets.

The variable *supplier distance* has been transformed into three separate items: national, European, and non-European purchasing volume. Only with an increase in the European purchasing volume, SSM adoption is encouraged. An intermediate distance to suppliers is related to higher levels of SSM. The cause may be a trade-off between risks and costs: A higher distance to suppliers implies higher risks but also higher costs. If suppliers are very close, the management of sub-suppliers possibly can be delegated to them, as there more likely exists a good relationship and trust (Choi and Krause 2006). If suppliers are far away, it is likely far more difficult to identify their suppliers and to get in contact with them. Risk of noncompliance with the focal firm's requirements is higher, but costs of SSM are higher as well (Grimm et al. 2014).

*Public visibility* surprisingly had a negative coefficient in the regression analysis, opposed to the hypothesis. However, this effect is only significant in one of the models and should not be overinterpreted. Four reasons can be thought of: First, focal firms could be rather motivated to adopt SSM by customer requirements than by pressures from the general public. If customers are other businesses rather than end consumers, public visibility may be low and the extent of SSM nevertheless high. Second, high public visibility potentially rather stimulates investments into communication and public relations than in SSM. Third, high public visibility may only be a determinant of SSM if focal firms fear scandals, which presumably only rarely is the case. Fourth, public visibility could have been understood by respondents as being somehow similar to a good reputation, and a good reputation in itself is no reason to consider sub-suppliers.

Four determinants without any effect on SSM remain. They will shortly be considered in the following paragraph. As already mentioned, the extent of SSM varied significantly across industries, but this effect is not considered as relevant because of the low number of observations per industry. With a higher number of observations and/or a lower number of industries, most likely meaningful effects would be observable, as the industry variable controls for a variety of contextual factors as, for example, customer requirements, material criticality, public interest, regulations, the competitive situation, profitability, power structure, or pollution levels.

With regard to the legal form of focal firms, no significant differences in the extent of SSM between stock corporations/limited liability companies and other types of firms have been found. Stock corporations/limited liability companies potentially differ in their strategic orientations compared to other types of firms, but as SSM results from a variety of strategic orientations, stock corporations may implement SSM because of different reasons than other firms or SSM practices may differ, but the overall extent of SSM is not affected.

The fact that the variable *sustainability-oriented turnover share* (SOTS) turned out to be irrelevant for SSM may be due to a very heterogeneous sample with regard to industries. Sustainability or fair-trade claims may be evident in some industries, as, for example, the food industry, and not relevant at all in other industries. In addition, the question asking for sales figures resulted in lots of "don't knows," as participants likely do not have exact information or the information is confidential.

Lastly, channel power has no effect on SSM. This can be attributed to the complexity of the construct "power." Channel power may entail opposite effects: On the one hand, a focal firm with high channel power can better enforce its SSM practices, and therefore a successful SSM is more likely (Grimm et al. 2016). On the other hand, powerful focal firms might more easily delegate responsibilities to their direct suppliers and thus refrain from SSM.

## 6 Outlook

The question if SSM contributes to genuine sustainability improvements in supply chains was discussed in Sect. 3. A simple answer to this question does not exist, but participation, transparency, accountability, and long-term collaboration were identified as criteria which help to assess specific SSM initiatives with regard to their contribution to supply chain sustainability.

Which insights have additionally been generated by the survey? The bad news first: sustainability commitments of focal firms are only subordinate as a reason to engage in SSM. A reputation orientation, among other reasons, is more important. There is evidence that sustainability commitments are closely related to the motivation to avoid reputation problems, respectively, to gain a positive image. The critique uttered by NGOs like Oxfam or the Clean Clothes Campaign that standards and audits—which according to the survey are among the most popular SSM practices—serve rather at soothing customers' or shareholders' consciences than leading to substantial amelioration of working conditions and environmental protection in supply chains is legitimate. The prevalence of SSM practices for sub-supplier assessment rather than for sub-supplier collaboration among surveyed firms insinuates that the establishment of long-term partnerships with sub-suppliers only happens in exceptional cases. However, there are good news as well: SSM is incompatible with a strategic focus on cost reduction and delivery performance (yet, these good news are quite limited: both strategic orientations are strongly favored by most of the participants). Hence, there is hope that despite the points of criticism with regard to standards and audits, SSM represents a countermovement to a business practice which puts suppliers and sub-suppliers under cost and time pressure and which is judged as the source of sustainability problems in supply chains (Preuss 2005; Wilshaw 2010). In addition, the fact that ethical and image considerations are not the only motivations for SSM, but first and foremost strategic orientations on quality, innovation, and risk management, could be a "selling point" for NGOs that want to promote sustainability initiatives in supply chains. They can seize firms by their core economic interests and bring the competitive advantages that result from a sustainable SSM to the fore, using claims such as "win-win situation" and "creation of synergies." However, it is strongly questionable in how far counting on the economic interests of firms for the dissemination of sustainable management practices leads to genuine sustainability improvements, or if it only contributes to a further dilution of the idea of sustainability. In any case, promoting SSM is not enough if eco-fair value chains are to be achieved before it is too late, even if firms claim to manage their sub-suppliers because of a sustainability commitment. It is a step in the right direction if firms focus on long-term instead of on short-term economic success. But above all, political frameworks are needed which secure the ecological and social limits within which economic activities must happen. Research on sustainable supply chain management should not presuppose that "profits are the ultimate assessment of supply chain performance and that managers and shareholders are the most important stakeholders in a supply chain" (Pagell and Shevchenko 2014). Instead, researchers should base their work on a definition of sustainability which includes the principles of intra- and intergenerational justice and the recognition of a maximum capacity and resilience of ecosystems. The critical question should not be "does sustainability pay?" but "how to create supply chains that are sustainable" (Pagell and Shevchenko 2014). For such an endeavor, research should not be limited to the (profit-driven) managerial perspective but should include the interests of less well-represented stakeholders such as workers in countries of the Global South or communities affected by supply chains.

## References


Aachener Stiftung Kathy Beys 2005–2018 (2015) Lexikon der Nachhaltigkeit|Wirtschaft|Drei Säulen Modell. November 18. Retrieved May 16, 2018, from https://www.nachhaltigkeit.info/artikel/1_3_a_drei_saeulen_modell_1531.htm

Awaysheh A, Klassen RD (2010) The impact of supply chain structure on the use of supplier socially responsible practices. Int J Oper Prod Manag 30(12):1246–1268

Bouchery Y, Corbett CJ, Fransoo JC, Tan T (2017) Sustainable supply chains: introduction. In: Sustainable supply chains. Springer, Cham, pp 1–12

Bowen FE, Cousins PD, Lamming RC, Farukt AC (2001) The role of supply management capabilities in green supply. Prod Oper Manag 10(2):174–189

Burger P (2015) Nachhaltige Entwicklung: Ein neues gesellschaftliches Paradigma? Retrieved from https://adam.unibas.ch/goto_adam_crs_313139.html
Burger P, Christen M (2011) Towards a capability approach of sustainability. J Clean Prod 19 (8):787–795
Burger P, Burkhardt-Holm P, Krysiak FC (2011) Educating experts for sustainable development: the master's degree in sustainable development at the University of Basel. In: Au Miroir des Disciplines: Réflexions sur les pratiques d'enseignement et de recherche inter- et transdisciplinaires = Im Spiegel der Disziplinen: Gedanken über inter- und transdisziplinäre Forschungs- und Lehrpraktiken. Lang, Bern, pp 133–153
Carter CR, Rogers DS (2008) A framework of sustainable supply chain management: moving toward new theory. Int J Phys Distrib Logist Manag 38(5):360–387
Carter CR, Rogers DS, Choi TY (2015) Toward the theory of the supply chain. J Supply Chain Manag 51(2):89–97. https://doi.org/10.1111/jscm.12073
Choi TY, Krause DR (2006) The supply base and its complexity: implications for transaction costs, risks, responsiveness, and innovation. J Oper Manag 24(5):637–652
Clean Clothes Campaign (2005) Looking for a quick fix: how weak social auditing is keeping workers in sweatshop. Retrieved from https://cleanclothes.org/resources/publications/05-quick-fix.pdf/view
Dobson A (1996) Representative democracy and the environment. In: Democracy and the environment. Edward Elgar, Cheltenham, pp 124–139
Eisenegger M, Schranz M (2011) CSR—Moralisierung des Reputationsmanagements. In: Handbuch CSR. VS Verlag für Sozialwissenschaften, Wiesbaden, pp 71–96
Elkington J (1994) Towards the sustainable corporation: win-win-win business strategies for sustainable development. Calif Manag Rev 36(2):90–100
Fawcett SE, Magnan GM (2002) The rhetoric and reality of supply chain integration. Int J Phys Distrib Logist Manag 32(5):339–361
Fox T, Vorley B (2004) Stakeholder accountability in the UK supermarket sector. Final Report of 'Race to the Top', IIED. http://www.racetothetop.org/documents/RTTT_final_report_full.pdf
Fuchs D, Kalfagianni A, Havinga T (2011) Actors in private food governance: the legitimacy of retail standards and multistakeholder initiatives with civil society participation. Agric Hum Values 28(3):353–367
Garland Mahler A (2017) What/Where is the global south? https://globalsouthstudies.as.virginia.edu/what-is-global-south
Grefe C, Zimmermann F (2018) Am Gängelband der Mächtigen. ZEIT
Greenpeace-Kampagne: Kitkat – Süßes mit bitterem Beigeschmack (2010) Retrieved April 30, 2018, from https://www.greenpeace.de/themen/waelder/kampagne-kitkat-suesses-mit-bitterem-beigeschmack
Grimm JH, Hofstetter JS, Sarkis J (2014) Critical factors for sub-supplier management: a sustainable food supply chains perspective. Int J Prod Econ 152:159–173
Grimm JH, Hofstetter JS, Sarkis J (2016) Exploring sub-suppliers' compliance with corporate sustainability standards. J Clean Prod 112:1971–1984
Grober U (2013) Die Entdeckung der Nachhaltigkeit: Kulturgeschichte eines Begriffs ([Aktualisierte u. erw. Neuausg.]). Kunstmann, München
Hofstetter JS (2016) Towards a process framework for sub-supplier management. Acad Manag Proc 2016(1):15827
Jeurissen R (2000) John Elkington, Cannibals with Forks: the triple bottom line of 21st century business. J Bus Ethics 23(2):229–231
Krause DR, Pagell M, Curkovic S (2001) Toward a measure of competitive priorities for purchasing. J Oper Manag 19(4):497–512
Kumar R, Singh KR, Shankar R (2014) Strategy development by Indian SMEs for improving coordination in supply chain: an empirical study. Compet Rev 24(5):414–432
Leppelt T (2014) Sustainability beyond boundaries. In: Sustainability in supply chains. Springer Gabler, Wiesbaden, pp 9–31. https://doi.org/10.1007/978-3-658-02601-1_2

Loske R (2016) Politik der Zukunftsfähigkeit : Konturen einer Nachhaltigkeitswende. FISCHER Taschenbuch
McWilliams A, Siegel D (2000) Corporate social responsibility and financial performance: correlation or misspecification? Strateg Manag J 21(5):603–609
Mena C, Humphries A, Choi TY (2013) Toward a theory of multi-tier supply chain management. J Supply Chain Manag 49(2):58–77
Pagell M, Shevchenko A (2014) Why research in sustainable supply chain management should have no future. J Supply Chain Manag 50(1):44–55
Pagell M, Wu Z (2017) Business implications of sustainability practices in supply chains. In: Sustainable supply chains. Springer, Cham, pp 339–353
Peters ML, Zelewski S (2013) Competitive strategies their relevance for sustainable development in the food industry. J Manag Sustain 3:148–157
Porter ME (1989) Wettbewerbsvorteile : Spitzenleistungen erreichen und behaupten (Sonderausg.). Campus-Verl, Frankfurt/Main [u.a.]
Preuss L (2005) Rhetoric and reality of corporate greening: a view from the supply chain management function. Bus Strateg Environ 14(2):123–139
Public Eye (2018) Rana Plaza – Fabrikeinsturz in Bangladesch—Public Eye. Retrieved April 30, 2018, from https://www.publiceye.ch/de/kampagnen-aktionen/eiaktionen/rana-plaza-fabrikeinsturz-in-bangladesch/
Rogers M (2004) Networks, firm size and innovation. Small Bus Econ 22(2):141–153
Sarkis J, Zhu Q, Lai K (2011) An organizational theoretic review of green supply chain management literature. Int J Prod Econ 130(1):1–15
Schaller S (2007) The democratic legitimacy of private governance: an analysis of the ethical trading initiative. INEF—Institut für Entwicklung und Frieden
Schnell R, Hill PB, Esser E (2013) Methoden der empirischen Sozialforschung, 9., überarb. Aufl. Oldenbourg, München
Seele P, Gatti L (2015) Greenwashing revisited: in search of a typology and accusation-based definition incorporating legitimacy strategies. Bus Strateg Environ 26(2):239–252
Smith BG (2008) Developing sustainable food supply chains. Philos Trans R Soc B Biol Sci 363 (1492):849–861
Starmanns M (2007) Fairness in globalen Wertschöpfungsketten durch Governance-Netzwerke? Wuppertal papers
Tachizawa EM, Wong CY (2014) Towards a theory of multi-tier sustainable supply chains: a systematic literature review. Supply Chain Manag 19(5/6):643–663
Terlaak ANN (2007) Satisficing signaling: corporate social strategy and certified management standards. Acad Manag Proc 2007:1–6
Vonderembse MA, Tracey M (1999) The impact of supplier selection criteria and supplier involvement on manufacturing performance. J Supply Chain Manag 35(2):33–39
WCEP (1989) Our common future. Retrieved April 30, 2018, from http://www.un-documents.net/our-common-future.pdf
Weiber R, Mühlhaus D (2014) Strukturgleichungsmodellierung: Eine anwendungsorientierte Einführung in die Kausalanalyse mit Hilfe von AMOS, SmartPLS und SPSS, 2nd edn. Gabler Verlag, Berlin
Werner-Lobo K, Weiss H (2006) Das neue Schwarzbuch Markenfirmen: die Machenschaften der Weltkonzerne; [der Globalisierungs-Bestseller komplett aktualisiert; mit neuen Facts, neuen Firmen und neuem Zündstoff!], Aktualisierte Ausg., 1. Aufl. Ullstein, Berlin
Wilshaw R (2010) Better jobs in better supply chains. Oxfam Policy Pract Priv Sect 7(1):1–20
Wuppertal Institut (2008) Zukunftsfähiges Deutschland in einer globalisierten Welt: Ein Anstoß zur gesellschaftlichen Debatte (4.). FISCHER Taschenbuch, Frankfurt am Main

# Digitalization and Sub-supplier Management

**Carsten Vollrath**

**Abstract** Many opportunities and risks are arising from the digital transformation of the industry. This chapter gives an overview over the key drivers of the digitalization as well as the key characteristics, elements, and current trends of a digital supply network. Core competencies for digitalization are discussed. Implications for the management of digital supply networks are derived, and the influence of new technologies on alliances and collaborations throughout the supply chain is evaluated. The use of blockchain technology as an enabler of collaboration in supply chains is discussed, and directions for future research are given.

The increasing digitalization has transformed the industry as we know it to industry 4.0. Hence, many opportunities and risks are imposed on companies. These include the easing of transaction management with customers as well as other business partners, since communication can be done in a fast manner. Furthermore, payments are now pursued digitally, and thus, there is no need to hold cash in another currency if a firm does business in foreign markets. Nowadays, high flexibility and a fast-paced environment characterize markets. Therefore, competition is increasing and is becoming more harmful to mature firms since the costs for setting up a business, i.e., in the online business, are extremely low.

However, the changes affect customers, too. Accordingly, it is cheaper to compare products and prices via the internet, which lowers the search costs tremendously. Furthermore, clients are demanding highly customized products in order to maintain loyal to a brand.

Especially influenced by digitalization and the imposed changes is the manufacturing industry. Undoubtedly, companies in highly industrialized countries are facing severe pressure form global competitors, arising in emergent economies, who benefit from production sites in low tax environments as well as low labor costs. Thus, they have been able to close the productivity and quality gap. In order to

C. Vollrath (✉)
Swiss IPG Partners Group AG, Schwyz, Switzerland
e-mail: c.vollrath@swiss-ipg.com

© The Author(s), under exclusive license to Springer Nature Switzerland AG 2021 
W. Stoelzle, J. Burkhardt (eds.), *Sub-Supplier Management*, Contributions to Management Science, https://doi.org/10.1007/978-3-030-75575-1_7

maintain or increase success in the current market position, it is necessary for well-established firms to strengthen the bond with its suppliers and, especially, the pre- or tier-n suppliers. Moreover, there is a need for decision-making in terms of outsourcing production steps in the supply chain in the future (Brettel et al. 2014).

# 1 Digitalization/Industry 4.0 and Supply Chains

## *1.1 Introduction*

Besides changes in markets and the overall competitive environment, supply chains are highly affected by digitalization and Industry 4.0 through the technological foundation of either concept (see Fig. 1).

Therefore, the implementations of IT in manufacturing businesses are key drivers for the growing speed at which every firm, market, and country is being revolutionized (Drath and Horch 2014). In this case, the focus is put on lowering the costs at which a communication infrastructure can be built. Thus, businesses are moving away from distinct operations to integrated networks, comprising many other firms, i.e., the suppliers and pre-suppliers, when using diverse technologies to communicate (Brettel et al. 2014). Consequently, a company is able to adjust its supply chain directly to the dynamic changes in the environment, i.e., fluctuations in demand, since information about products or parts as well as the current situation of its suppliers is now visible and thus can be analyzed. Moreover, concepts like the Internet of Things or artificial intelligence gain in importance, because machines may become able to generate knowledge or so-called intelligentization in the future. Therefore, it is necessary to implement digitalization and intelligentization into the manufacturing industry in order to enhance the level of product design, processes, and the overall management (Zhou 2013).

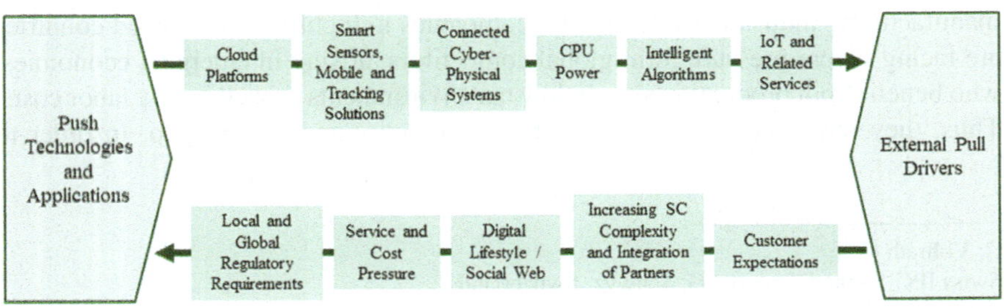


**Fig. 1** Technologies' push and demand's pull on the digital supply chain (PWC 2016)

## 1.2 Key Drivers of Changes in Supply Chains

In general, the changes in the supply chains are driven by many factors (Lasi et al. 2014; PWC 2016):

(1) Time

(a) Thus, the periods for development as well as production need to become shorter to stay competitive. Therefore, a manufacturer is forced to monitor every single step in the production in order to reduce the time to market.

(2) Individualization

(a) Due to increasingly blurred boundaries between suppliers and buyers, it is now possible to tailor the necessary materials, services, or products to the clients' wishes directly. Consequently, this influences not only the first-tier supplier but also every other upstream participant because those need to focus on every customer's preference.

(3) Flexibility

(a) Because of (1) and (2), manufacturers and suppliers must support an agile business model, which is able to leave room for quick changes to satisfy the buyer as well as downstream customers relentlessly.

(4) Decentralization

(a) Thus, (1), (2), and (3) need a clear and unrestricted communication infrastructure to ease the decision-making process. However, this is only possible if hierarchies are reduced and the flow of information is unconditional.

(5) Efficient Use of Resources

(a) Lastly, the increasing speed in the entire supply chain as well as dynamic changes in terms of demand and counterparts, focus should be put on sustainability. Meaning, that resources are chosen under aspects of economical as well as ecological efficiency. Accordingly, businesses must consider actions to increase their corporate social responsibility.

(6) Automation

(a) Since Industry 4.0 increases the adoption of mechanisms that automatically optimize several steps in the production process, distinct and isolated tasks as well as employees are replaced in the future.

(7) Digitalization and Networking

(a) Hence, the growing amount of data and supporting tools eases the implementation of internal as well as external networks to control and analyze the overall operations.

(8) Miniaturization

(a) Due to the utilization of technologies, a tremendous amount of space can be saved in facilities while increasing performance simultaneously.

## *1.3 Digitalization of the Supply Chain*

Traditionally, supply chains are characterized by a linear process, which involves the designing, planning, manufacturing, and delivery of a certain product (Deloitte 2016). As said before, those structures are broken up and connected to outside partners in the resulting digital supply network (DSN). Thus, it becomes easier for managers to enhance the performance, due to technologies, that are used to optimize the supply chain and, hence, monitor the volatility, volume, velocity, and visibility. Additionally, such developments are beneficial for all participants, because they oppose lower costs in terms of computing, storage, and consequently, increasing the overall success. Moreover, the costs of doing a transaction with partners in the supply chain decreases, which leads to the opportunity to divide one's energies to more suppliers. It means that the amount of simultaneous activities, i.e., information gathering and sourcing, is growing due to the high predictability and interconnectivity of the network (see Fig. 2).

The utilization of a supply network helps companies to exploit assets in many different ways because of diverse characteristics (see Fig. 3).

Those distinct functions enable activities that support continuous growth for each party. However, in order to exploit them, it is vital for any business to incorporate the DSN into its business strategy. Therefore, clear goals as well as objectives must be set, in order to maintain focus throughout the tremendous amount of different solutions and paths, which can be taken in the future.

Besides the already utilized core capabilities, there are many other solutions to optimize the flow of information and increase transparency through mature

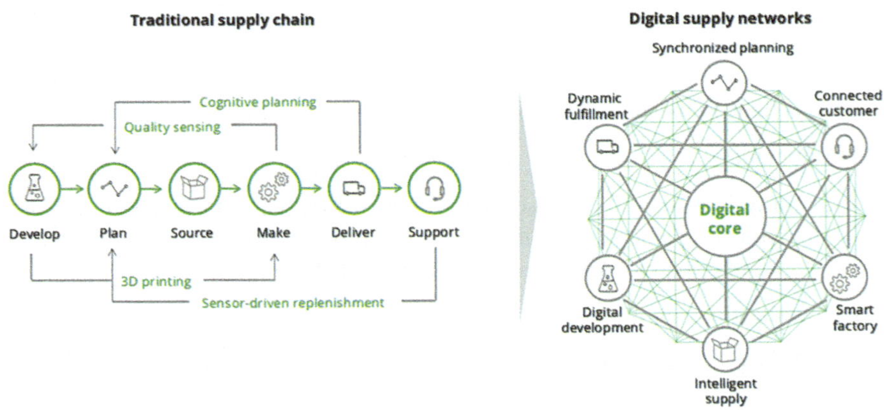


**Fig. 2** Shift from traditional supply chains to digital supply networks. Source: Authors' own illustration

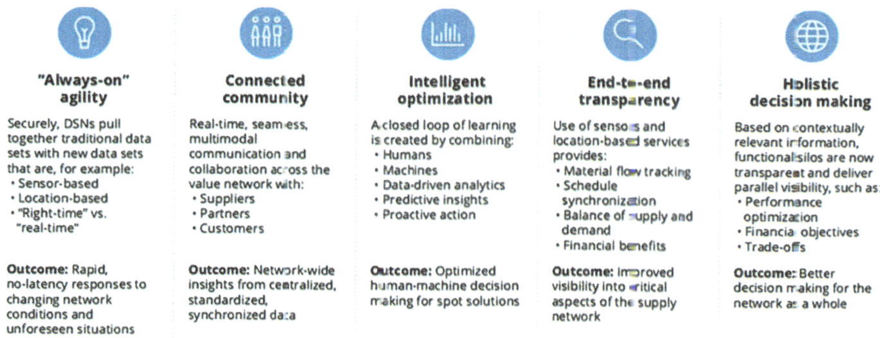


**Fig. 3** Characteristics of a digital supply network (Deloitte 2016)

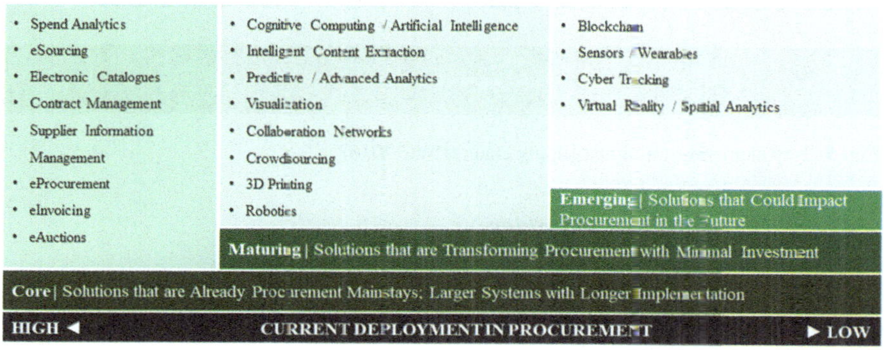


**Fig. 4** Deployment of core, mature, and emerging capabilities in procurement (Deloitte 2017)

technologies as well as upcoming new trends, i.e., block chains or virtual realities (see Fig. 4).

Consequently, the application of technologies in the entire supply network can support the decision-making and overall efficiency, because even external data about suppliers, i.e., tier-n, and other happenings can be enriched through digitalization and, thus, optimize mature practices on each step (see Fig. 5).

As a result, the planning and execution tasks are integrated in the platform, in order to exchange relevant information between the supplier as well as the buyer in real time. Thus, all strategic actions, involving the overall operations, tactics, and optimization of the sourcing strategy, are now adjusted regularly throughout the entire process and not only annually or semi-annually.

One of the main pillars of digital supply networks is transparency, because the occurrence of hearsay is diminished through real-time news feeds about weather conditions, political as well as traffic situations, and many more. Therefore, risky steps like packing or shipping become extremely certain since every centimeter a part or module makes is documented and accessible for every participant.

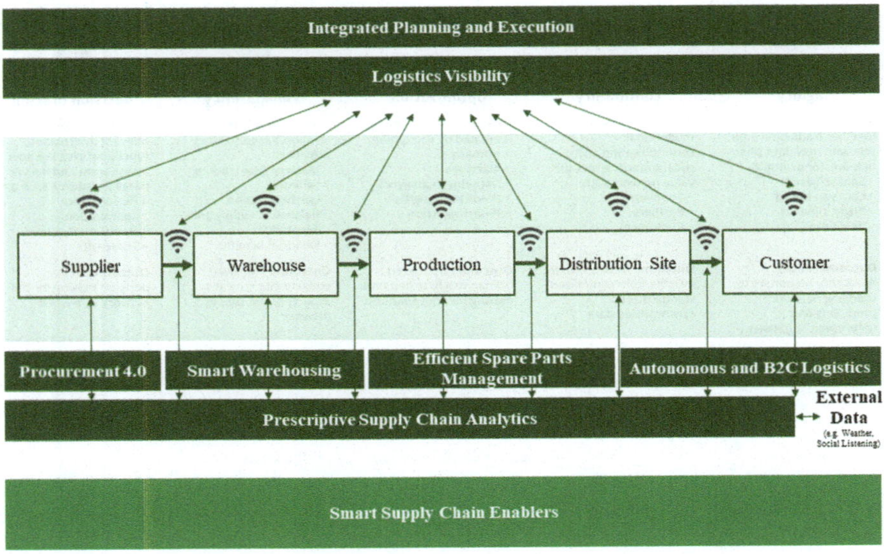


**Fig. 5** Key elements of a digital supply chain (PWC 2016)

## *1.4 Necessary Competencies*

In order to benefit from technological mechanisms or collaborations, several competencies are said to be highly important to form networks in the supply chain. Accordingly, only if those capabilities are met, each participant is able to control its operations efficiently, reach its individual strategic goals, and overcome the imposed challenges.

Thus, to generate value from a network, materials and products need to be identifiable and locatable in every step of the supply chain over their entire life cycle. Additionally, personal competencies are necessary to increase the autonomous processing of tasks through flexibility. Furthermore, employees must have social skills to secure a constant flow of information to other involved divisions or the supplier along standardized supply chain steps. Moreover, an agile mindset is demanded, which concerns the ad hoc finding of solutions to concur shortcomings in the value chain. Thus, managers take the role of mediators in internal and external relationships, supporting unrestricted cooperation throughout the entire network. Further, it is important to leave enough room for individual ideas, not only internally but also from upstream actors, which lead to more overall efficiency. Consequently, managers must be able to breakdown complex concepts into different steps, while considering the individual risks, in order to divide them among the collaborative network to successfully exploit a "brownfield" route or explore a totally new "greenfield" approach (Erol et al. 2016) (Fig. 6).

Besides internal capabilities, there are many non-network-related competencies, which should be considered, too. Thus, mechanisms and tools must be chosen and

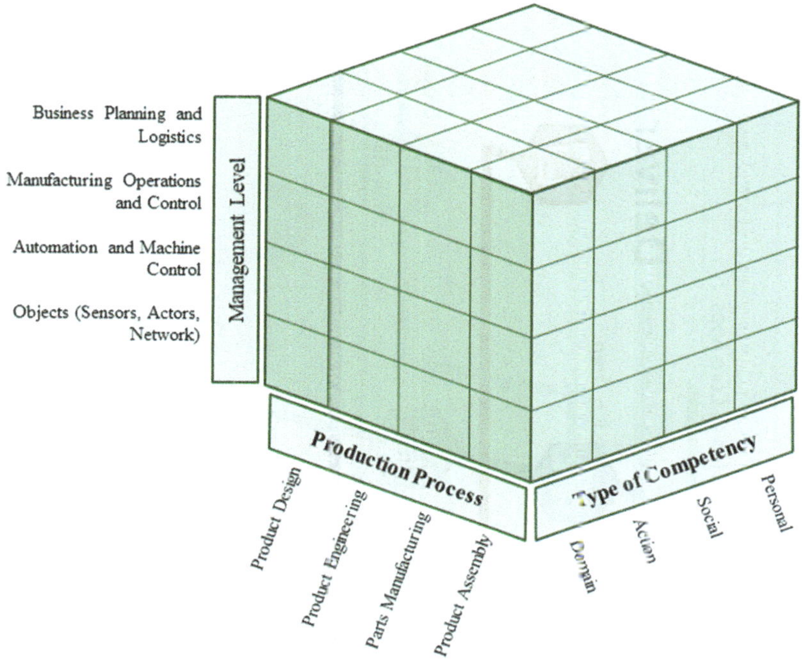


**Fig. 6** Problem area-competency cube (Erol et al. 2016: 17)

applied effectively. For instance, the utilization of machine-related data can help to shape the supply chain to fit the businesses' individual needs, but only if the right methodologies are used and interpreted correctly (Erol et al. 2015).

## *1.5 Implications for the Management of Digital Supply Networks*

Besides the extreme benefits, which appear in digital supply chain networks, managers should begin to focus on the responsiveness of each participant. Especially, upstream suppliers need to be monitored more carefully, since their products are vital for a constant flow of profits. Thus, the first step towards easing the changes considers adjustments of the business model because this is the only part managers can actually change and impact (Bode and Wagner 2015).

Accordingly, upcoming trends must be understood and implemented to stay competitive in the future (see Fig. 7).

For instance, in the case of transportation management, DSN's can help a manager to plan, control, supervise, and finally analyze the operations in a timesaving manner, because every step is becoming visible. In this case, a clear

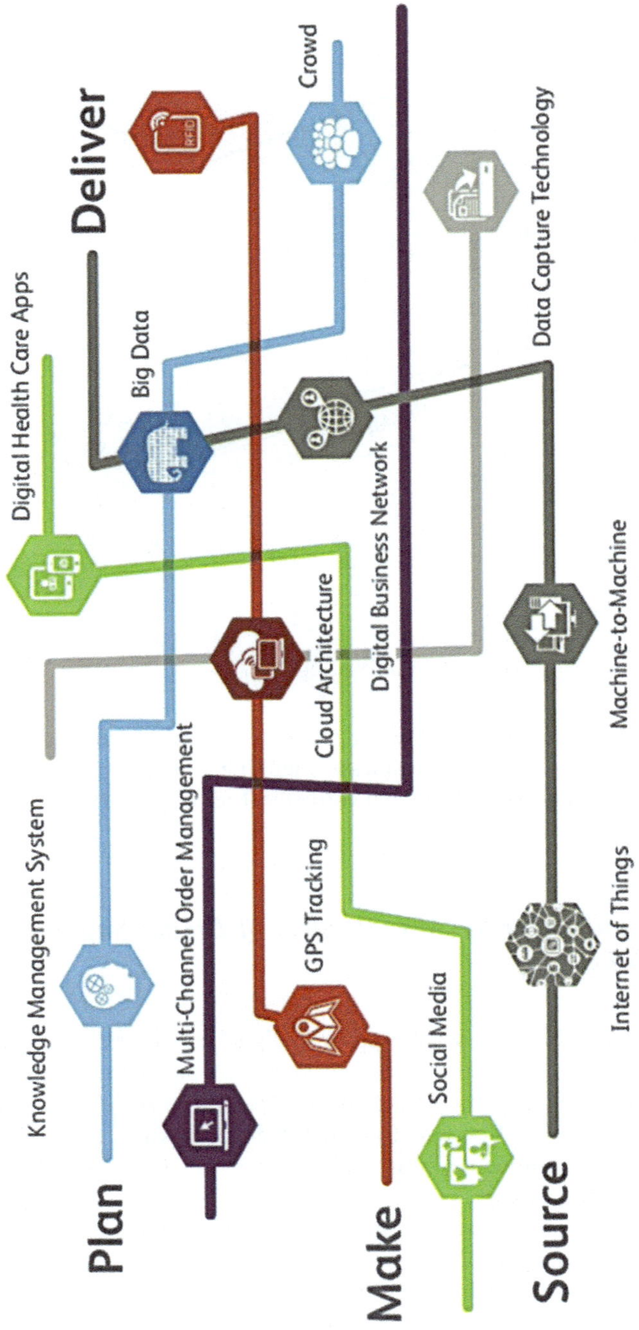


**Fig. 7** Digitalization trends in supply chain management (Bearingpoint 2016)

digital strategy must be developed, starting with the identification of the internal digital infrastructure and how it could be applied to the different supply processes, followed by the stating of different measures to make the outcomes reliable in terms of numbers and profitability. In the end, certain steps may be prioritized and selected in order to draw a roadmap for future improvements (Bearingpoint 2016).

## *1.6 Challenges*

In order to undertake the alteration in the supply chain through digitalization, there are some obstacles that must be overcome. Especially, the extreme interconnectivity with outside partners is in some points highly critical, because a company must disclose sensitive information throughout its network. Thus, mechanisms to improve the data security as well as privacy are necessary to protect the owner's and the suppliers' specific know-how. Similar to this are technologies which can prevent unauthorized access to production systems or other facilities by an outsider (Drath and Horch 2014). Consequently, any technology must be reliable in terms of control and safety applications, because if a firm fails to do so, it might lose its competitive advantage in the future (A.T. Kearney and WHU Logistics 2015)

Considering the utilization of wireless communication, it is especially vital to decrease the latency. This means that a company and its suppliers must choose a wireless network which is able to serve enough coverage to support an instant communication. In comparison to that are the costs that incur while using technologies. Obviously, such systems consume energy and need to be synchronized regularly, which leads to an increase in the communication overheads (Varghese and Tandur 2014).

Continuing with the challenges imposed in terms of the supply chain in general, which combines internal and external partners, it is necessary to build modular factory structures that inherit many smart devices, i.e., cyber-physical systems, which can secure a consistent exchange. In order to do so, standardized actions must be developed to ease the cooperation between technical providers and every member of the supply chain (Weyer et al. 2015). Such standards involve (1) electro-mechanical as well as (2) communication functions. This means that all hardware, software, and modules, used somewhere in the supply chain, must be compatible with the previous or latter participant. As far as proper communication standards are concerned, it is vital to utilize the same type of data as well as systems under which the highly digitalized machines and members are able to communicate throughout the network (Weyer et al. 2015).

# 2 Applicability of Technologies in Supply Chains (Upstream)

## 2.1 Complexities in the Upstream Network

Besides the positive aspects, there are many complexities when it comes to upstream supplier relationships. Thus, the interconnected flow of materials, modules, information, and funds imposes risks to businesses, because of disruptions in the network (Bode and Wagner 2015).

Such supply network disruptions are defined as discrete events, which cause losses for the participating businesses and, thus, interrupt the regular flow of operations (Bode and Wagner 2015). For instance, if a tier-n supplier is not able to deliver an important part to the latter on time, the manufacturer as well as the end customer cannot be delivered either. This results in the loss of profits and reputation.

However, those disruptive events occur through complexities in the overall network, which are either structural or operational. Structural complexities arise due to the number of connections and participants in the digital supply network. So, when the number of tier-n suppliers rises, a manufacturer as well as the first-tier supplier has to increase the information gathering in order to secure transparency. Additionally, more technologies need to be implemented to adjust either party to the end user' needs, while operational complexities describe the direct interactions between every element of the system. Accordingly, digitalization gives many opportunities to overcome the former, but it also increases the number of interactions with suppliers, who are further up in the network. Those must be monitored very carefully through adjusted mechanisms in order concentrate one's energies on the profitable solutions. Furthermore, business models need to be aligned to the complexities, since more hierarchical levels exhibit greater problems than organizations that have fewer (Bode and Wagner 2015).

## 2.2 Alliances and Collaboration Throughout the Supply Chain with the Help of Technology

Due to the change of supply chains towards digital supply networks, it is important to understand the necessity of alliances as well as collaborations throughout the system in order to overcome the risks and challenges. Generally, supply chains and procurement relationships are characterized by asymmetric innovation. This problem has now been able to be offset due to more transparency, imposed by information technologies, which also offer many innovative opportunities in the future (Pramatari 2007). Subsequently, this leads to an increase in the overall success as well as profits. For example, a big car manufacturer uses a product life cycle management software to connect its production teams all around the world to incorporate different inputs for a design. That is, the disclosing of specific tasks to a broader group of diverse people leads to a better solution in the end.

However, for a supply chain collaboration to be successful and of length, several factors which determine the success and lifetime of a partnership need to be considered (Ramanathan and Gunasekaran 2014).

In today's business world, the planning is highly different due to the increasing number of relationships. Therefore, manufacturers must introduce a collaborative approach, i.e., to get in contact with a logistics and replenishment provider or for the purpose of sales promotion and product design. However, most activities are now concerning the sharing of information, and thus, collaborative planning involves the adjustment and improvement of visibility among all participants in the supply chain. Undoubtedly, precise planning mechanisms increase the overall collaborative success (Ramanathan and Gunasekaran 2014: 6). In order to make the collective planning efficient, the information that is exchanged needs to be in a coherent format, i.e., XML or DTD, because this will enable the tier-n suppliers to enter new and receive updated information simultaneously. Major breakthroughs to ease those tasks are third-party online platforms, e.g., e-marketplaces in the grocery industry (Pramatari 2007: 211 f.). Those make it easier to get in contact with not only one but also multiple upstream partners at the same time to exchange information and conduct business. Similarly, a buyer can increase the legal compliance of its products and parts which are delivered by the suppliers on each tier. Again, this saves time and costs and makes the supply chain more efficient in the long run, because the occurrence of faulty pre-products or parts is extremely reduced. Conclusively, the ease of connecting to tier-n providers gives the chance of making every transaction, internally and externally, leaner.

Subsequently, the processes in terms of production and replenishment are executed collaboratively, too. Since it becomes possible to pool inventories or stock jointly, large cost savings for every partner can be generated. For instance, a pre-supplier can now follow the information exchange between the other upstream partners and is notified about the amount of stock the latter has left in real time and, thus, can adjust its replenishment to the latter's needs. This will in turn reduce the number of bottlenecks throughout the entire supply chain, which is beneficial to all participants, and support the collective success, respectively (Ramanathan and Gunasekaran 2014). Additionally, profits can be increased for the network, if decisions are made in cooperation, e.g., when all partners are able to decide on the sales price. Therefore, the demand can be controlled, especially in promotional or discounted sales, since it is easier to forecast on the one hand and, thus, make quicker changes to one's inventory and replenishment plans on the other (Ramanathan and Gunasekaran 2014).

In general, it can be said that collaboration between a manufacturer and an upstream supplier is more successful when activities in terms of planning and decision-making are carried out together. However, a prosperous partnership will not necessarily result in future collaborations, because there are many other factors that need to be considered (Ramanathan and Gunasekaran 2014: 6).

### 2.3 Integration and Management

Especially considering the transparency in terms of upstream activities, it has been proven that alliances in a supply network have extremely positive effects on the invention success, because either party can benefit from the opponent's technologies and knowledge (Dutta and Hora 2017). However, such relationships are highly dependent either on management or, on entrepreneurial activities and capabilities.

In order to benefit from a partnership, either business has to negotiate on the kind of contract that should set the guidelines for the operations, considering three different contracts between an upstream supplier and the downstream manufacturer (Wang and Shin 2014):

(1) Wholesale Price Contracts

The wholesale price contract is the most used mechanism in any supplier-buyer relationship, because it leaves the manufacturer with enough freedom to focus on maximizing its profits and afterwards calculating the price it is willing to pay for the needed parts. Hence, with the growing usage of technologies that generate a highly informative environment throughout the network, a business receives the opportunity to find cheaper vendors or information about the pre-suppliers, which gives it more bargaining power in price negotiations, for example, if it finds out that the first-tier supplier is labeling the parts with "Made in Germany," but actually they are manufactured and put together in China.

(2) Quality-Dependent Wholesale Price Contracts

This type of contract implies specific quality requirements, and thus, a supplier is committed to source all materials at a certain quality level. This effort is then being compensated by a higher wholesale price. Such contracts are often used in industries where the quality of certain parts is vital for the overall success. For instance, when Apple began to design the iPad, it needed displays, which must have met certain requirements for the touch screens to work. Due to digital measurements, i.e., the pixel count, LG and other suppliers were not able to serve the needed quality and, thus, were exchanged by a different vendor. Accordingly, Apple was and still has a lot of influence on its upstream suppliers, even though it does not produce the final devices itself (Wang and Shin 2014).

(3) Revenue-Sharing Contract

This means that the generated revenue is shared after the final products reach the end customer. Thus, in a network, this is only beneficial for the suppliers, because they are able to receive a bonus on top of their charged production fees. Therefore, innovative activities are pushed, because of the increasing amount of payment, which should be maintained in the future. However, the principal business in the middle of the system is only getting a percentile out of its operations, which is unfavorable. Nonetheless, in the case of Apple, it used such contracts for apps, which it did not develop, because additional value could be added to the original devices.

## 2.4 The Use of Blockchains in the Supply Chain

Besides the collaborative approaches, which are highly beneficial when it comes to building a relationship to a tier-n supplier, another technology must be considered in the future of supply chain activities as well. In some cases, the information, which is shared between a manufacturer and its suppliers, is highly sensitive and, thus, needs to be protected against whistle blowing, when passing through the network. If a buyer is willing to pursue a decentralized supply chain approach, with the highly specific knowledge, the technology of blockchains comes into play.

Generally, blockchains represent distributed databases, which transport transaction-based data in a highly transparent, comprehensible, and validated manner. However, sensitive information is delivered to each network node in an encrypted format. Subsequently, the data block is checked for adequacy before new information is and can be added. This process ends with collecting all transactions on a block, which cannot be reversed in the future (IBM 2016: 8f).

One of the main benefits of using blockchains in supply chain transactions are the contracts, which are prepared for every possible event. Accordingly, if a situation occurs, the necessary steps are pre-stated and carried out automatically, i.e., a clear directory of property rights or the payments between participants without the necessity of a collateral. Due to the clear structure, it becomes easier to monitor previous actions and determine the origin of every single item and lower costs while sharing cargo holds for planes, trucks, and ships, because the information about status of loading is extremely accurate (IBM 2016). In addition to that, any product recall, due to false or damaged parts, can be carried out faster, since the provider of the insufficient module can be identified in only minutes.

Conclusively, the manufacturer, who is in need of a secure and stable supply chain, can identify pre-suppliers extremely fast, too. This is because of the high transparency and the forgery-proof information on the blocks, which is comparable to an accounting system that can be checked for previous data.

However, many blockchains are open for a large number of participants to enter, which can increase the overflow of information as well as the time that is needed to process the data, since none of the past transactions are deleted from the chain. Likewise is the preparation of smart contracts, which is done by real people, so mistakes or events might occur that were not explicitly stated in the agreements (IBM 2016).

In order to solve those issues, a supply chain network can make use of permissioned blockchains, since those restrict the number of nodes (participants) and, thus, the capacity and amount of information, which is exchanged during transactions. Furthermore, the security aspects of a permissioned network need to be considered, too. Therefore, an independent platform provider uses mechanisms in which participants need to sign up and authenticate themselves, making the blockchain transactions very attractive for highly specific relationships in a supply chain.

In order to benefit from blockchains, the network needs to foster trust by securing the information from flowing out. Additionally, a manufacturer might operate the blockchain with many different suppliers who are competitors. Therefore, there is a need for mechanisms to shield specific transactions from being viewed by other suppliers in the manufacturers' DSN. Moreover, general legal regulations must be adhered in the contractual agreements and any occurring action, in order to avoid difficulties with authorities. Last but not least, the systems need to guarantee smooth processes and a high quality of information (IBM 2016).

When all necessary characteristics are met, blockchains can be used throughout the supply chain for activities concerning, for instance, the (IBM 2016):

- *Monitoring* of needs and flows of raw materials in terms of pre-suppliers
- *Tracking* of information for any material, module, or product, which is passing through the supply chain
- Increasing of *automation* within the network, i.e., activities of replenishment
- *Optimizing* of cargo routes by reviewing and analyzing the business analytics

## 2.5 Upstream Supplier Competition

However, digitalization and the use of technologies, i.e., increased collaboration and blockchains, throughout a supply network can increase the success and efficiency on the one hand, but the upstream participants have to face a tremendous amount of changes in their competitive environment on the other.

Concerning the growth of bargaining power, which is handed to manufactures, severe implications on the provider side are imposed. Thus, their competitive pressure increases tremendously. Especially, tier-n suppliers are put under the pressure of delivering the highest quality materials at the lowest possible price. If they fail to do so, the manufacturer or the first-tier supplier can easily switch to another participant in the upstream network. This results in a monopolistic position of either parties, first-tier supplier or manufacturer, especially if a quality-dependent contract is used.

Another force of competition considers complementary components. Therefore, even other participants are affected by innovative activities of the main provider or other upstream actors. For example, if Apple is updating the software of its devices, every supplier in the network, i.e., application developers, needs to adjust to the changes in order to maintain the compatibility of parts or services and to lower the risk of being exchanged (Wang and Shin 2014).

## 2.6 *Questions for Future Research*

- Governance rules of the new digital supply network infrastructure
- How many partners and connections are suitable/efficient and at what point is the information overflow or the number of complexities too high to be managed?
- Do the relationships between a manufacturer and its tier-n suppliers differ from industry to industry?
- Is the structure of "tier-xy" suppliers even necessary in the future, since it might become possible for a manufacturer to approach the necessary partners directly and pursue the other steps by itself, since information becomes more symmetrical?
- Are blockchains an alternative for industries which are based on integrity and trust?

# References

A.T. Kearney, WHU (2015) Digital supply chains: increasingly critical for competitive edge. A.T. Kearney, WHU Logistics

BearingPoint (2016) Digital transformation in supply chain management. BearingPoint

Bode C, Wagner S (2015) Structural drivers of upstream supply chain complexity and the frequency of supply chain disruptions. J Oper Manag 36:215–228

Brettel M, Friederichsen N, Keller M, Rosenberg M (2014) How virtualization, decentralization and network building change the manufacturing landscape: an industry 4.0 perspective. Int J Inf Commun Eng 8(1):37–44

Deloitte (2016) The rise of the digital supply network- industry 4.0 enables the digital transformation of supply chains. Deloitte

Deloitte (2017) Digital procurement- new capabilities from disruptive technologies. Deloitte

Drath R, Horch A (2014) Industrie 4.0: hit or hype? [industry forum]. IEEE Ind Electron Mag 8 (2):56–58

Dutta D, Hora M (2017) From invention success to commercialization success: technology ventures and the benefits of upstream and downstream supply-chain alliances. J Small Bus Manag 55 (2):216–235

Erol S, Jäger A, Hold P, Ott K, Sihn W (2016) Tangible industry 4.0: a scenario-based approach to learning for the future of production. Procedia CIRP 54:13–18

IBM (2016) Fast forward: rethinking enterprises, ecosystems and economies with blockchains. Blockchain. IBM Institute for Business Value, pp1–28

Lasi H, Fettke P, Kemper H, Feld T, Hoffmann M (2014) Industry 4.0. Bus Inf Syst Eng 6 (4):239–242

Pramatari K (2007) Collaborative supply chain practices and evolving technological approaches. Supply Chain Manag 12(3):210–220

PWC (2016) Industry 4.0: how digitalization makes the supply chain more efficient, agile and customer-focused. PWC

Ramanathan U, Gunasekaran A (2014) Supply chain collaboration: impact of success in long-term partnerships. Int J Prod Econ 147:252–259

Varghese A, Tandur D (2014) Wireless requirements and challenges in Industry 4.0. In: International conference on contemporary computing and informatics (IC3I). IEEE, pp 634–638

Wang J, Shin H (2014) The impact of contracts and competition on upstream innovation in a supply chain. Prod Oper Manag 24(1):134–146

Weyer S, Schmitt M, Ohmer M, Gorecky D (2015) Towards industry 4.0: standardization as the crucial challenge for highly modular, multi-vendor production systems. IFAC-PapersOnLine 48 (3):579–584

Zhou J (2013) Digitalization and intelligentization of manufacturing industry. Adv Manuf 1(1):1–7

The manufacturer's authorised representative in the EU is Springer Nature Customer Service Centre GmbH, Europaplatz 3, 69115 Heidelberg, Germany. If you have any concerns regarding our products, please contact ProductSafety@springernature.com

Printed and bound by CPI Group (UK) Ltd, Croydon, CR0 4YY
30/09/2026
02225467-0010